A Dance to Freedom

Your Guide to Liberation from Lies and Illusions

Sylvie Imelda Shene
with Ed Sweet

Published in the United States of America
by Sylvie Imelda Shene.

Sylvie Imelda Shene is available for speaking engagements. To make arrangements, please write to sylvie@sylvieshene.com.

Second edition
ISBN-10: 1539859886
ISBN-13: 978-1539859888

10 9 8 7 6 5 4 3 2

*This book is dedicated
to my enlightened witness*

*Alice Miller
1923–2010*

*"It is not true that evil, destructiveness,
and perversion inevitably form part of
human existence, no matter how often this
is maintained. But it is true that we are
daily producing more evil and, with it, an
ocean of suffering for millions that is
absolutely avoidable. When one day the
ignorance arising from childhood
repression is eliminated and humanity
has awakened, an end can be put to the
production of evil."*

— Alice Miller, *Banished Knowledge*, p. 143

Contents

Foreword

Sylvie Imelda Shene can see what happened to people as small children. She can also predict their futures. She's not psychic or clairvoyant, but she knows that people unconsciously and compulsively tell the true and traumatic stories of their childhoods by repeating, reenacting and recreating them in the present moment.

Sylvie realized this was happening to her, and to everyone around her, when she became a devotee of Alice Miller in the year 2000 at the age of 41. Miller, a Swiss psychologist, achieved worldwide renown in the 1980s and 1990s for her books about how the repressed emotions of childhood traumas can have a huge influence on the course of our lives, forcing people into a state of compulsive repetition that keeps them stuck in childhood without knowing it.

Miller's writings intrigued Sylvie from the day she started reading them. And ultimately, Miller's work became the only thing that could free Sylvie from her emotional prison and save her from an abusive relationship with a man named Marty. Marty was a Leonardo DiCaprio lookalike who Sylvie met when she was a topless dancer in the 1990s — a job she turned into a lucrative career that spanned nearly 18 years.

Unlike the typical guy who approached Sylvie at the strip club where she worked, Marty forced Sylvie to break all her rules. And he triggered all the painful feelings from her early years of being unwanted, emotionally abandoned and neglected by the people closest to her.

Sylvie did everything she could to win Marty's love and affection, from forgiving his affairs and feeding his drug habits to buying him a $7,000 Honda VFR750F sport touring motorcycle. She knew she was in a sick place, but Marty had gained complete control over her.

Sylvie turned to self-help books and a 12-step program for guidance, hoping to become the loving person who could get Marty to change. It was a reference in a book Sylvie was reading — *Codependents' Guide to the 12 Steps* by Melody Beattie — that led Sylvie to Alice Miller's *Thou Shalt Not Be Aware: Society's Betrayal of the Child.* Sylvie knew just from the subtitle that she had found something important. Sylvie read the book and liked it, but set it aside because she was hoping to get a quick fix from her Al-Anon group.

Four or five years later, when Sylvie and Marty's relationship was at its worst, Sylvie was brought to her knees — not to be taken to God as her 12-step program prescribed, but to finally confront the reality of the repressed child she once was. Sylvie returned to the works of Alice Miller, refusing to be distracted by groups that only gave the illusion of love and an empty promise of salvation. She read *Thou Shalt Not Be Aware* again, along with all of Alice Miller's other books.

This time, Sylvie realized how she was unconsciously and compulsively reenacting her childhood drama — not only with Marty, but also with members of her 12-step group and just about everyone else she had relationships with. Alice Miller became Sylvie's "enlightened witness," — in the sense of truly knowing how to heal — and helped Sylvie truly feel the intense feelings of the repressed child she once was for the first time in her life.

I met Sylvie some five years ago on Facebook. She attracted my attention through comments about Alice Miller that she posted on her blog and on her Facebook page, Facing Childhood Traumas. I first learned about Alice Miller in the 1980s, when I was a young university student of education in Hamburg, Germany. In Alice Miller's books, I found for the first time — expressed so clearly and with great empathy by a professional — what, by means of intuition, I had always felt when I watched adults interacting with children. Something was going deeply wrong in those relationships!

Alice Miller's deep insights into the human mind and heart have accompanied and supported me throughout my life as a mother and a teacher. When I met Sylvie, I felt that she was one of the few other people who had not only read Alice Miller's books, but also had really understood her teachings far beyond the intellectual level. Like myself, Sylvie let Alice Miller into her heart and thus was able to heal from her traumatic experiences.

I'd like to thank Sylvie for being brave and strong enough to share her life with us in this fascinating and inspiring book. I hope her words will make it around the world and into the hearts of many readers. *A Dance to Freedom* isn't just another typical "self-help" book. It's the story of an amazing woman who shows us how to break away and heal from severe childhood traumas.

Petra Helm
Huesca, Spain
2014

One Friday after the bar closed, the manager asked us girls if anyone wanted to work at Bourbon Street on Sundays. Back in the mid-1980s Bourbon Street was the hottest "gentleman's club" in Phoenix, Arizona. The same people who owned Cheetah One — where I worked — also owned the much larger and lively Bourbon Street and they let us work there on Sundays when Cheetah was closed. I decided to give it a try and it was a huge improvement: The club was filled with fun young college guys and I was doubling my money by making $400 a night. Naturally, I didn't want to go back to Cheetah. So on Monday I went to talk to Bob, the good-looking manager at Bourbon Street who was the same age as I was. I liked Bob. But I didn't like the nasty general managers who eventually went to jail for racketeering and extortion. I pleaded my case to Bob in his office, unaware that the creepy general managers were in the next room, listening to my every word. The older one, a little man in his sixties, burst into Bob's office and got all up in my face. "You are a Cheetah girl first and you can only work here on Sundays," he spat at me. "I am no Cheetah girl," I said. "I am no Bourbon girl. I am nobody's girl. If I can't work here, I'm not working for you at all." I left them speechless as I walked back to my car, but I was trembling inside. What the hell did I just do? Now I was going to have to look for another job and it would be hard to find anything that paid as well and was so much fun. As I was getting into my car, I felt a tap on my shoulder. Bob had this silly grin on his face as he told me, "If you want to work here, show up tomorrow night at 6:00."

Introduction

I worked as a topless dancer at the Bourbon Street gentleman's club in Phoenix, Arizona, from 1985 to 2003, from the time I was 26 to the time I was 44. Eighteen years is a long time to be in that particular field — especially when you get as late a start as I did — but dancing was the perfect career for me. I made a lot of money. I got paid to stay in shape. And I got a lot of attention from a reasonably well-behaved group of male college students, movie stars and professional athletes. There's nothing wrong with a little flirting, right?

More than most of the other girls, I was able to approach dancing as just a job. I was simply putting on a show, and I had no need for messy emotional entanglements. I wanted to work hard, have a little fun, earn my money and go home at the end of the day like anyone else. When I was working as a dancer the clubs were actually pretty innocent. The girls only went topless, and up until the year 2000 the patrons had to stay at least 12 inches away from us. Physical contact was strictly prohibited.

There were a few other girls like me who approached dancing with a good head on their shoulders. But most of them moved on after college, or when they got married or pregnant. They danced for the money and it was usually a short-term arrangement. And then there were the girls who got caught up in all sorts of craziness, from drugs and prostitution to very serious physical abuse at the hands of the "sugar daddies" they were desperately looking for.

Many times while working at Bourbon Street, very well-dressed men would come in and try to entice us girls with promises of fame and fortune. Whenever someone told me they wanted to make me a movie star, I just smiled at them and thought to myself, "Yeah right, probably a porn star!"

Sometimes groups of dancers would leave the club with visiting celebrities to party in their hotel rooms. It used to drive me crazy when these famous guys would fall for dancers who played them just to get their money, even to the extreme of trying to get pregnant. It's so unbelievably sad that anyone would create another human being just to be a tool for manipulation. Back then I tried to keep my distance from everyone, and I treated the rich and famous guys just like anyone else. They were just regular customers to me and, as far as I was concerned, they could look elsewhere if they wanted special treatment.

I only hung out with celebrities a couple of times, usually to test the love of my boyfriend Marty. The experience I remember the most was with Charlie Sheen when he was at the height of his career in 1991 — after movies like *Platoon*, *Wall Street* and *Major League* made him a superstar.

When Charlie came to the club all the dancers swarmed around his table. I honestly didn't even recognize him. I knew he had to be some kind of hot shot though, judging by all the attention he was getting. When I was on stage he noticed me and came up to where I was dancing. He gave me a $50 tip and asked me to dance for him at his table. I told him he'd have to wait because I had already promised dances to some other guys. He was visibly stunned.

"Don't you know who I am?" he asked.

"No," I replied. "Should I?"

He let out a nervous laugh and asked me to come dance for him when I had a chance.

When I fulfilled my obligations to the other customers, I went back to Charlie's table. "Are you ready for my dance now, or do you want me to come back later?" I asked.

"Yes, I'm ready," he said. "Please dance for me."

As I was dancing, he asked me if I was sure I didn't know who he was.

"Someone just told me you're a movie star," I said. I took a good look at him and added, "You do look familiar, but the person I'm thinking of looks a lot older than you do."

"You're thinking of my dad," he said. "Have you ever seen *Platoon?*"

"Isn't that a war movie?" I asked. "I'm not much into war movies, but now that I've met you I promise I'll rent it this weekend."

He really couldn't figure me out, but he invited me back to his hotel. To ease my mind, he mentioned that a lot of the other girls were going. I thanked him for the invitation and said that I'd think about it. I finished my dance for him and told him I had other customers waiting.

At the end of the night he sought me out and asked me if I was coming along to party at the resort. "I'm still thinking about it," I said with a smile. He told me that his group was going to grab some breakfast at a nearby diner first, and that I should join them there. If I didn't like it, I could just go home after that.

I agreed to meet him at the restaurant. When I got there he was in the middle of a large corner booth, surrounded by about ten dancers. It was like a scene out of a movie! While we were eating, Charlie kept asking if any of the dancers could score some cocaine.

"Don't look at me," I said. A few of the girls got up to make some calls — there weren't any cell phones in those days — but it seemed like all of the drug dealers in Phoenix were out of the stuff everyone was looking for. Charlie paid the bill at the diner and once again asked me to come to his hotel.

I was definitely curious about what kind of party it was going to be, so I said I'd go for a little bit. As soon as we arrived at his suite, the alcohol started flowing. Charlie was on the bed with a harem of dancers, and I sat a safe distance away on a sofa with another girl. Some of the dancers kept looking for coke, and by 3:00 a.m. it arrived. Charlie got all happy as people started snorting lines.

I was starting to get a little uncomfortable, so I got up to get some water. Charlie followed me and asked me to sit next to him. I smiled. Part of me wanted to let loose a little bit, but there were just too many girls around. So I sat back down on the sofa next to the other dancer. Out of nowhere she gave me a huge kiss, right on the lips. I don't know if she did this because she liked me or because she wanted to turn Charlie on. Either way, I have to admit that it was kind of exciting. It was my first and only kiss from a woman and I still remember how soft her lips were.

I thought to myself that I had better leave the resort before things got out of control. I got up and thanked Charlie for his hospitality and told him that I had to go. He tried to convince me to stay, and so did my new girl crush, but I just couldn't do it. Plus, I think the other girls from Bourbon Street were happy that I was leaving. I could tell that they were holding back a little because I was there. I had a reputation of being somewhat of a prude with the other dancers. Deciding to let them have their fun, I picked up my purse and went home to my cats.

Dancing at Bourbon Street gave me a fascinating window through which to view human behavior of all kinds — the good, the bad, the beautiful and the ugly. I saw a lot of girls pull themselves out of a lot of difficult circumstances, but I also saw a lot of people crash and burn. I saw love, compassion, hatred, abuse and even murder.

As weird and as dangerous as the world around me could get sometimes, I always tried hard to stay above it all. And even though everyone knew that I was pretty conservative, I did my best not to judge what I heard about the things other girls did at the club or on the side. If someone wanted to be a "dancer/prostitute" or a "waitress/prostitute," that was their business. However, I never understood how some of the waitresses could have a problem with dancing, but were perfectly fine having sex for money.

In all my years as a dancer, only one girl was completely honest with me about her extracurricular activities. I appreciated her candor, and when she had a relationship problem I was happy to let her crash at my house for a few days. The whole time I listened to her project all her hatred into men. Man bashing was a favorite pastime of most of the dancers, which I found kind of ironic because they were being paid to please people they absolutely despised. I couldn't have done my job if I blamed men in general for my problems. Frankly, I think that's a copout.

For me, keeping my nose clean at Bourbon Street was a good decision. I didn't want to get used up by getting involved with gambling, drugs or a futile search for a sugar daddy like so many of my colleagues did. Besides, dancing always made me feel free. I enjoyed being able to move. I liked to flirt a little bit. And it was no problem for me to enforce a policy of not dating the customers.

That is, until Marty came around. He was a Greek god. An Adonis. A Leonardo DiCaprio clone whose cool vibe and raw animal magnetism drove every girl at Bourbon Street wild. Marty could have had any dancer he wanted, but he chose me. It was probably because I was so hard to get, and I have to admire him for his persistence. He pursued me for nearly a year, and I finally succumbed to his charms by telling him he no longer had to pay me to dance for him. Since he was no longer a customer, we could start dating.

For a variety of reasons my relationship with Marty ranks among both the worst and the best experiences of my life. Even though he was 11 years my junior, Marty had a strange effect on me in more ways than one. Our relationship was passionate and intense, and the sex was like something out of the *Kama Sutra*. When I could lose myself in the ecstasy of our physical acrobatics, I was in heaven. But the rest of the relationship was a living hell.

As I would eventually discover, Marty managed to trigger all of the pent up emotions I had repressed as a neglected child. My reactions to his numerous affairs — and his ultimate rejection of me for someone else — were repeat performances of struggles I had had with my parents, siblings and other authority figures who had control over me as a young child.

Of course, I didn't know this at first. I didn't know why I was so hopelessly attracted to Marty, even though he was a womanizer who took advantage of me every chance he got. I didn't understand why I kept going back for more and more of his mistreatment. I had no idea why I kept buying him expensive presents or lending him money for drugs. It really didn't make sense why his love and approval mattered so much to me. I'd been dumped before — and I had dumped my share of guys, too — but none of my romantic relationships had ever been this overwhelming.

Just as I did when I was little, I tried to fix things. I tried to fix Marty. I tried to fix myself. I tried just about everything — from therapy and 12-step groups to Oprah-style forgiveness and positive thinking — but nothing worked. I was in utter despair because I just couldn't find a solution. I didn't know that the answer was already inside me, in the memory of the little girl who was treated in the same cruel way by her parents, her sisters and brothers, and her teachers.

I got a glimmer of hope one day when I started reading a book by Alice Miller. This remarkable woman — a renowned psychologist and author of 13 books — literally changed my life. Her ideas about how people repress traumatic experiences that occur in childhood — and then relentlessly repeat them in their adult interactions — spoke to me more clearly than anyone or anything else had ever done.

Alice Miller made me feel that I wasn't alone anymore. She showed me that the cause of my fear and pain wasn't Marty after all. He was just a trigger of the intense feelings of hurt and anger I kept locked away, which were never allowed to find true expression when they first occurred. The real causes of my problems were the repressed emotions of the little girl I once was. And she demanded attention in the here and now.

One of the reasons I love Alice Miller so much is because she's the only person I've encountered on this planet who was 100 percent honest, courageous and real. She sticks to the facts and doesn't preach to anyone. She tells it like it is.

Her words taught me to see how the pressure to create a false self as a child — in order to cope with the crazy adults in my life — was damaging me as an adult. She explained how I had become a prisoner of my childhood. And she guided me through a powerful journey that freed me from the consequences of old wounds.

My list of childhood traumas was pretty long. In fact, I had just about every disadvantage in life that you could think of. I grew up in a poor village in Portugal, the daughter of a drunken father and an exhausted mother who never got over the death of three of her ten children. I was the youngest child in my family and I was born when my oldest sibling was 25. By the time I came around, the last thing my parents, brothers and sisters wanted was another mouth to feed.

I was very delicate as a baby, and very vulnerable to illness as a young child. I nearly died of hepatitis when I was seven years old. That episode was so bad that I had to spend an entire year at home when I should have been starting school. I was a burden on the family and the focus of great resentment.

When I finally started school other issues came to the surface, including a severe learning disability. My inability to do schoolwork was another embarrassment to my family, and it gave the harsh Catholic teacher who led my class conniption fits. Let's just say she acted in a very unloving way toward me, which reflected very poorly on the religious teachings of her church. At an early age, organized religion turned me away from God. Religion felt like a straitjacket keeping me down. Just like Alice Miller, I was "unable to fathom God's motives," and, in my own way, came to the same conclusion she did, that the God of the Bible was perverse and cruel.

"The Bible was written by men," Alice Miller writes. "We must assume that those men had been through some unpleasant experiences at the hands of their fathers. Surely none of them had had a father who took pleasure in their inquiring minds, realized the futility of expecting the impossible of them and refrained from punishing them. That was why they were able to create an image of God with sadistic features that did not strike them as such. God as they saw Him devised a cruel scenario in which He gave Adam and Eve the tree of knowledge but at the same time forbade them to eat its fruit — that is, to achieve awareness and become autonomous personalities. He wanted to keep them entirely dependent on Him."[1]

My difficulties were especially problematic in a family that claimed to value religion and education above pretty much everything else. I was the one kid in the family who wouldn't tow the line and behave the way I was supposed to. I was wild at heart with an expansive spirit. And to my parents and older siblings who were responsible for taking care of me, this spelled trouble with a capital "T."

Throughout my childhood, family members told me that I wasn't good enough, smart enough or polite enough. I never did the right thing. Under the strict rule of two of my sisters, Elza, the oldest child, and Laura, the third oldest, I acted out by being rebellious and withdrawn. These sisters — my substitute parents — were exasperated with my behavior. When their efforts to control me through harsh words, humiliation and even medication failed, they pretty much rejected me and made their displeasure with me even more widely known.

By the time I was a teenager I was in emotional turmoil.

Like most children ruled by authoritarians, I was forced to repress my true feelings and believe that I was the problem. My caregivers ignored my childhood feelings in an effort to gain the upper hand, and I believe that's true of most people raising children today. Alice Miller taught me that children tend to idealize the people who are supposed to love them, even when they don't. It's a coping mechanism that children use because they can't afford to face the truth of not being loved when they're so young, vulnerable and unable to survive on their own.

---

[1] *The Truth Will Set You Free*, p. 7–8

Everyone around me reinforced the idea that I was the one who was wrong, which led me to resent my sister Isabel. She was three years older than me and was also raised by Elza and Laura, who constantly held her up as the model of perfect behavior. She was the heroine of the family and I was the villain. I didn't know then that Isabel's obedience and compliance were just her ways of coping with the same oppressive authority figures. Just recently, Isabel complained to my sister Elza that she was jealous of me because my illnesses and bad behavior kept stealing the spotlight from her when we were kids.

I can imagine that Isabel felt extremely traumatized when she saw our mother pregnant with me, this new baby who would take her place. Isabel was only three when I was born and no one was available to help her deal with her feelings. So she developed her own false self, which made her do everything she could to please adults in order to get their attention. It worked as a child, but as an adult she's stuck in her own emotional prison, perpetuating the vicious circle and passing it on to the next generation. Until she frees herself to start down the path toward her true self, she'll continue taking refuge in delusions of grandeur that hurt everyone around her.

Elza and Laura may have meant well when they were raising me, but all their efforts were geared toward making me something I was not. Truth be told, I wasn't even that bad of a kid! I was a hard worker and very disciplined, but because I wasn't book smart and didn't believe in God, my positive qualities were overlooked.

If my substitute mothers had just tried to meet me where I was, things may have worked out differently. Instead, they constantly picked on me, told me that I'd never be good at anything and made it clear that I was ultimately going to hell. Once they even got an old friend of theirs to remove the "bad spirits" that had taken over my body! When that didn't work they turned to one of Portugal's leading psychotherapists, a dashing young doctor who today is a national hero, kind of like Dr. Phil is in the United States. All this doctor seemed to want from me was a blow job, and I went along just to spite my sisters. I'll tell you more about this Prince Charming later.

As a result of a collection of bad experiences that were never acknowledged, explained or discussed, I was pretty much a hot mess when it was time to enter the real world.

For a while, I was able to escape my family and the emotional hold they had on me. I went to London to work as an au pair, and ultimately moved to the United States on a fiancée visa. When my friend backed out of the marriage plan, I got hitched to another guy I had met in London. The problem with him was that he really wanted to be my husband. I was very honest with him about not wanting a relationship, but he seemed to think we'd be able to work it out.

A year after getting married I got a divorce and moved to Phoenix, Arizona. In Arizona's urban heart, I found my calling at Bourbon Street. And then, five years into my career, I met Marty. While I was in that relationship I thought I was on a rollercoaster ride from hell, but looking back it was an incredible journey of discovery — thanks to a lot of help from Alice Miller and her wonderful books.

Alice Miller helped me see that there's only one true way to achieve freedom. This requires really feeling the repressed emotions of childhood for the first time. Children can't process the fact that their parents were incapable of love, so they learn to deny the truth in an effort to survive. They create an illusion of love when they're young, but this illusion can be severely damaging if it doesn't jibe with reality.

However, as adults, we all have the potential to reclaim our truth and free ourselves from lies and illusions.

I'll be very honest with you: Following my path to freedom wasn't an easy process for me. As Alice Miller writes, "Inevitably, resistance to following this path is great, as we all fear our repressed past and the experience of how helpless we once were. We have had good reason to be afraid; if we did not, there would have been no need for repression. Yet the more we encounter our fear and dare to see its causes, the more it decreases."[2]

When I was finally ready to face my repressed rage and fear — after years of reading Alice Miller and absorbing her teachings — it took me months of being a virtual recluse before I was able to push through the pain and find myself free on the other side. It felt like my chest was being ripped apart by a knife, and I can't tell you how many boxes of Kleenex I went through. But as hard as it was, I'm a much better person for having faced — and felt — my true feelings. Today, I'm much happier and it's very hard to rattle me. Freedom has a price, but it's totally worth it.

If I didn't have Alice Miller to help me connect the dots and understand the real roots of my pain, at some point I probably would have shut down completely. In fact, I had already shut down when I was a little girl in order to survive, and I tried to commit suicide on more than one occasion. The raw pain buried deep inside me, which was triggered years later with great intensity when Marty finally left me, was my opportunity to wake up and become fully alive again.

After spending ten years with Marty I finally became too smart for him. Gone were the days when he could manipulate and fool me. I was no longer willing, or able, to live with his lies and be his secret. He either had to get real

---

[2] *The Drama of the Gifted Child* (1994), p. 25

with me or leave. And because he couldn't be honest and truthful, he split. Being left by this man, who was just like my dad in that he couldn't stand up for himself or for me, forced me to face and feel the raw pain of being emotionally abandoned and unloved as a child.

I was able to find genuine forgiveness and understanding by acknowledging what was really done to me as a child, and by gaining insights into why my parents, sisters and others couldn't help doing what they did. As Alice Miller says, "Such forgiveness cannot be coerced by rules and commandments; it is experienced as a form of grace and appears spontaneously when a repressed (because forbidden) hatred no longer poisons the soul."[3]

If you haven't guessed it already from my career choice, I'm the type of person who naturally attracts — and for the most part likes — attention. And I don't just mean that in a sexual way. Wherever I am, I seem to be able to strike up a conversation with anyone who crosses my path. I'm perfectly willing to talk to people and help them out if I can.

In my exchanges with men and women from all walks of life, I've found that so many of us remain lost little children, looking and waiting for a substitute mother or father figure to save us. But that can never happen because no one can make up for what we didn't get when we were young. As adults, we have the ability within ourselves to finally become a loving mother or father to the lost child still inside us, with the help of an enlightened — or knowing — witness. Alice Miller was mine.

Ignoring our childhood truth, Alice Miller says, "makes us act destructively even though we do not really want to do

---

[3] *For Your Own Good*, p. 248

so."[4] Some people become abusers, lashing out at others (especially their own children) because they couldn't confront their own oppressors. Some people become pros at manipulating others, using illnesses caused by their unresolved childhood emotions to get people to take care of them like their parents never did. And some people, like me, simply let the repressed emotions of the child they once were sabotage their lives when stressful situations come up.

Before Alice Miller died in 2010 I was lucky enough to have had an email correspondence with her that lasted about two years. She wrote to me once that the rage of an adult — who attacks others out of a denial of his or her history — can never be resolved because it's directed at scapegoats. She told me that therapists who don't allow patients to confront their childhood feelings are actually doing great harm. "Staying trapped in the hatred toward scapegoats can't be the successful end of therapy," she wrote to me. But the expression and release of legitimate rage, directed at the real abusers, can be the beginning of a successful life.

This is why all of us need a path — or a dance, if you will — to freedom. Once you explore your truth, incredible things can start to happen. Chronic symptoms, mental as well as physical, can start to disappear. As Alice Miller writes, we can "claim health, clarity and independence for ourselves. Claim them, and maintain them. Only thus can we keep our feet on firm ground, and not be dependent on drugs, gurus, groups or theories that teach us how to change our past."[5]

The dirty little secret is that we can't change the things that happened to us. But we can find the courage to face them, mourn our past and move forward. If a person like me — with no formal education or special talents — can do it,

---

[4] *The Drama of the Gifted Child* (1994), p. 9

[5] Ibid., p. 13–14

then you can, too. This book, along with all or any of Alice Miller's books, can be an enlightened witness that helps you with your own dance to freedom.

When I started corresponding with Alice Miller in the last years of her life, I told her that I wanted to help her spread the word about her discoveries. No one who wants the truth should have to wait as long as I did. And that's why I wrote this book. It's both a tribute to Alice Miller and a guide to her ideas. I'm not a therapist, and I don't want to be anyone's therapist. But I do want to help people as a friend would, by sharing my experiences and explaining how Alice Miller helped me heal when everything else failed.

If you struggle with anger, resentment, depression, addiction, disease or a bad relationship, Alice Miller can help you gain what you missed as a child — "truthfulness, clarity and respect for yourself and others."[6] I've done a lot of the legwork for you, and if you can learn from my story you can avoid many of the mistakes I made during my own dance to freedom. You can find your freedom a lot sooner than I did.

It's time to liberate yourself from the victim role you fell into as a child when you lacked the resources you needed to take care of yourself and stand up to your oppressors. I'm living proof that Alice Miller's ideas work. And I'm happy to share my dance to freedom with you in the hope that it inspires you to start your own.

---

[6] *The Drama of the Gifted Child* (1994), p. 26

Most of the girls at Bourbon Street weren't able to make enough money just dancing. They were always working on some scheme behind the scenes, or were trying to find a sugar daddy to live off of for as long as they could. Most of the time, the dancers I knew were broke because they spent all their money on drugs, shopping and who knows what else. I approached the job differently and always had money. I was very aware that someday it would all be over. While the money kept flowing in, I wanted to save as much of it as I could so I'd never have to be dependent on anyone. I was the only dancer I knew of who had any credit cards — and I had all of them! I just loved collecting them because it gave me a sense of independence. I wouldn't use them much — only for small things or in an emergency — and I always paid the balances in full. Most of the other dancers liked having me around because I was so responsible. They could always rely on me to get them out of a jam. Sometimes they'd get in big trouble and come to my house crying. One girl came over at 3:00 a.m. dripping wet because she was chasing her boyfriend and crashed her car into a canal. I'd let these wayward souls stay with me for a while until things settled down. I became a loving mother figure to more than a few of the girls, who saw me as being genuine, real, truthful and understanding.

1. Trauma

It's been half a lifetime since I saw my seven-year-old sister Zita on fire. I was just two years old and was playing at home with Zita and Isabel, who was five. Our brother Carlos was supposed to be watching us, but he left us alone in the house to help a man from the village who was having engine trouble. In my family we were all told to put our own needs aside in order to help others. And since Carlos was a better mechanic than he was a babysitter, it seemed only natural to him to put a seven-year-old in charge of us while he left to look at the machine.

Nobody heard our screams as the horrifying flames engulfed Zita's dress. She had ventured too close to the fireplace in an attempt to prevent the fire from dying so we could stay warm. When her dress caught fire, Zita ran through the house like a blazing fireball and Isabel and I followed her like complete maniacs. By the time my poor sister careened through the hallways and somehow managed to extinguish the flames that surrounded her, she had suffered severe burns all over her face and body. After an agonizing few days in the hospital, Zita died.

Even though I really can't remember Zita, her untimely death has had a significant impact on me. My mother wore black for the rest of her life and remained in a constant state of grief. I remember going to the cemetery with my mother when I was a little girl, to visit the graves of Zita and a brother of mine who died in 1950. My mother talked about these two children of hers like they were perfect little angels. "If only they had lived, all of us would be better off," she would say. I would listen to her and feel her grief. I was angry at God for taking these perfect children away from my mother, who wore their cherub-like photos in a necklace every single day and would kiss their likenesses all the time.

Living in the shadow of the perceived perfection of our dead siblings was difficult for the rest of us. And years later, I'd gain insights into my mother's behavior and its effect on our family from Alice Miller: "Experience shows that the death of a child ... plays a very important role in a mother's life. The birth of every child inevitably awakens or reawakens desires in the parents that somehow are connected to making up for their own childhoods. Either they look to the child to compensate for their not having had good parents ... or to be the child they once were. If the child dies soon after birth, before the parents' expectations are disappointed by the child's desire for autonomy, the mother may idealize her lost child and thereby preserve its central importance for the rest of her life. Often after the death of an infant, there is no real period of mourning that runs its course: instead, the parents' hopes become attached to an 'if': if only the child had lived, the parents think, their expectations would have been met. The belief in the fulfillment of all their hopes, originating in their own childhoods, is associated with the memory of this child, whose grave they visit and tend for decades after." [The remaining children] must be dutifully cared for and raised in a way to rid them of their bad behavior and make them acceptable in the future. To be too affectionate would be dangerous, for too much love could ruin them ... And so the poor ... mother feels a duty towards her living children to train them well and to suppress their true feelings. But it's a different matter in the case of her dead child, for that child needs nothing from her and does not awaken any feelings of inferiority or hatred, does not cause her any conflict, does not offend her." [7]

My father handled his grief over Zita's death differently than my mother did. He went even deeper into the alcoholic haze that helped him cope with all of life's injustices. I have a

---

[7] *The Untouched Key*, p. 27–28

feeling that he retreated into drink not because his children died, but because of the way their deaths changed my mother.

My mother's constant grief and my father's amped-up drinking were just two of the more obvious signs of the helplessness and despair that perfect Zita and Antonio left behind them. But quite honestly, even without my sister being burned to death and my brother's head being crushed by a wheel from a farm cart, my family life in rural Portugal was pretty traumatic. We were poor. I was the youngest of 10 children. My mother and father were in an arranged marriage. My father was a drunk. And at the time Zita was being burned beyond recognition, my mother was actually visiting my brother Nuno at the hospital because he had been badly injured in a traffic accident. The deck was definitely stacked against us.

My mother and father were no strangers to abuse. My mother didn't get along with her parents, especially her mother, and one of her uncles tried to molest her when she was 15 years old. My father's father left when my father was still a young boy, and my father's mother died shortly thereafter. Abandoned and rejected by his real parents, my father was raised by a family friend. My father was a very depressed man. He drank almost every day to numb himself from the pain of his own childhood. As a consequence of his emotional unavailability, I was very neglected as a child. I grew up alone in an emotional desert, and I would repeat the pattern with the emotionally unavailable men I fell in love with.

My father supported us — and his drinking habit — as a government road worker, while my mother tended to the house and kids. She kept chickens and rabbits and other small animals, and maintained a large garden that produced most of our meals. It wasn't an easy life, especially with the family always growing. By the time I was born in 1959, my parents' marriage was strained to the breaking point and my father was drinking pretty heavily.

I'm actually surprised that my parents were able to stay together at all. My mother was pretty ticked off when her parents agreed to marry her off to this strange man. My father would go off drinking every night, and every night my mother would just lose it. Despite his addiction, however, I think my mother grew to like my father. I remember her saying many times that the only bad thing about him was his drinking. I think she always had the hope that if she could just get him to stop abusing alcohol, everything would be fine.

But my father never stopped drinking. It got so bad that people in our village would entertain themselves by buying drinks for him — just so they could laugh at him when he got wasted and when my mother got pissed off. One time I was with my father in the village bar, trying to get him to leave. I must have been only three or four years old. All the men were buying drinks for my father and laughing at him, while I kept grabbing his hand and pulling it so he'd go home with me. My father kept letting go of my hand to grab another drink.

I had to endure this rejection until the bar closed. Finally my father had to leave with me, but he was so drunk he could barely walk. To add insult to injury, some teenagers from the village laughed and threw rocks at us as we made our pathetic journey home.

As a young child, I had no choice but to repress the pain of this and many other experiences. Facing the painful truth of my parents' shortcomings at age three or four was incomprehensible. But until I could finally feel the pain caused by an emotionally blind father who preferred drinking with the men at the bar than going home with the little girl who loved him, I would remain a prisoner to the pain. I used to have crying spells when I was with my boyfriend Marty at sports bars. His desire to keep drinking with his friends rather than take me home triggered the repressed pain of having my love discarded by my father in a similar way.

As painful as my family dynamics were, much of the trauma swirling around me had little direct effect on me in my earliest years. I have fond memories of my mother protecting me in my first years of life. And despite my father's alcohol problem and inability to be present emotionally, he was never violent and never spanked me. He was gentle and kind when he was sober, and would often give me the food off his plate when I was hungry. I was actually a pretty happy child. And, for a few years, from the time I was three until the time I was seven, I was lucky to have had the full attention of my mother. All the other children were gone and would only come to visit on weekends and other special occasions. So, for a time, it felt as though I was the only one who mattered.

Some of my happiest memories are of helping my mother in her rose garden, smelling the magnificent flowers in the summer sunshine. We also shared long talks while we walked together to the village, where we would visit with my mother's friends or wash clothes at the river with a group of women.

I also remember many pleasant evenings sitting by the fireplace with both of my parents, listening to the radio and eating roasted chestnuts. Before my father had too many drinks, he would play with me and tell me stories. I always asked him to tell the tale of Maria da Fonte. She was a brave Portuguese woman from the province next to ours who started a revolution in 1846 against the corrupt local government. My father would sing her song to me and I have to say that his voice was very pleasing. He could be quite entertaining when he had only a couple of drinks in him.

Things started getting a lot worse for me by the age of seven when I was supposed to start first grade. I was eager to learn and excited to see what school was all about, but before I could even get to the classroom I contracted hepatitis and nearly died. I missed the entire year and had to start first grade again when I was eight years old, a full year older than the rest of the kids.

I soon realized how lucky I was to have been sick for an entire year when I finally went back to parochial school. My new teacher was an ignorant, hateful woman who called me lazy on a regular basis. She humiliated me in front of my younger classmates because I could never seem to give the right answers. I always understood my lessons, but I got nervous when I was called on. My teacher would hit my hands if she caught me counting with my fingers, and she hit me on the head with a stick when she was teaching me the alphabet and multiplication tables. Rather than try to help me, she resorted to ridicule. She seemed to take pleasure in trying to bring me to tears each day. My older sister Elza was this woman's teacher when she was a child, and I think she was taking revenge on me.

I'm not trying to excuse my teacher's behavior, but Portugal in and prior to the mid-1960s wasn't so kid friendly. Those were the last years Prime Minister Salazar's long dictatorship and there was a shortage of teachers — especially in rural areas like the one where I lived. To deal with the strain, children were allowed to leave school after the fourth grade — and many of these people somehow became teachers as adults. Classrooms were run with narrow-minded strictness just like the country was, and instructors were quick to pull out their rulers and hurl insults at innocent children.

I never gave my teacher the satisfaction of crying in front of the class. Instead, I repressed the pain and acted tough. I remember very well how I used to tighten my muscles to suppress my emotional pain. I was always tense and had a difficult time sleeping at night. My anxiety levels were so high that my stomach hurt.

School was extremely difficult for me, and nobody there or at home seemed willing or able to help me in any meaningful way. Years later I discovered that I had a severe case of dyslexia. Just identifying this condition as an adult allowed me to better understand myself and start letting go of the shame I felt as a child. But back when I was an impressionable first grader I didn't know what was going on. I lost my passion for learning and started skipping school every chance I got.

Things at home weren't much better for me. My battle with hepatitis and my struggles with school branded me as weak and dimwitted among most of my family members. My parents didn't know how to protect me from my abusive teachers. Mom and dad had a warped respect for people who were more educated than they were, so they simply expressed shame at my inability to get good grades. Everyone in the family started to blame me for my difficulties, as if I could have done something different at eight years old to correct the situation.

I was considered a burden on the household. While my mother was sometimes a safe haven for me, she was often too preoccupied with the loss of her precious Zita to console me. And my drunken father was too wounded by his own circumstances and failures to be emotionally available.

I went from being a pretty carefree child to getting caught up in a toxic environment that was eating away at my psyche and destroying my spirit. I did my best to cope with the trauma by developing a tough skin and a fierce independent streak, not realizing that in the process I was just repressing the emotions of an innocent and impressionable little girl who was teased viciously at school and emotionally abandoned by her family.

Like most children, I felt that I was somehow responsible for my problems. My parents certainly never sat me down and explained what was going on, or apologized for any of their actions. And no other authority figure in my life ever took any responsibility or tried to approach my problems in a different way. They took the easy way out and just blamed me for not being good enough.

The people around me all had their own traumas to deal with, and they weren't dealing with them very well. They were either crippled by them, like my mother, or escaping from them, like my father. Or they were denying that their problems even existed, like most of my siblings and the Catholic school faculty.

So there I was, young and vulnerable, unable to understand that the people who were supposed to guide me through life were actually laying the foundation for a path filled with problems that would haunt me for decades.

Before I started second grade, my sister Isabel and I were sent to the capital city of Porto to live with our two older sisters. Elza was 32 — more than a generation older than I was — and Laura was 28. They had moved to the city to work as nurses, and my parents thought that Isabel and I would get a better shot at life under their supervision. By my family's standards, my two eldest sisters had made it big. They pulled themselves out of poverty and seemingly overcame the misery of life in the village of Zoio by working hard and getting college degrees.

One summer day my mother put us on a bus, and Isabel and I took the eight-hour trip over rough roads to Porto. All I remember is falling asleep and then hearing Isabel announce our arrival. Out the window I could see the bustling port city, the streets crowded and noisy with cars and electric buses. Porto looked incredible to my young eyes and I was excited to be there. When Elza picked us up from the bus station we went straight to the beach, and I was thrilled by my first glimpse of the vast ocean. Elza was even nice enough to buy us swimsuits with polka dots and our own little purses. I chose red and Isabel picked the green one.

It seemed like this bright new beginning in a brand new place was just what I needed to leave my problems behind. But I would soon learn that it was all just another illusion. At the time we arrived in Porto, Elza and Laura were finishing up their internships at the hospital São João. They were staying in the nurses' dorm rooms and they sneaked us in to sleep in beds that weren't being used. One night, Isabel and I were left in the care of two other nurses. One of them asked me what grade I was in. I told her that I'd be starting second grade in the fall. For some ignorant reason, the other nurse asked me if I knew how much three plus two was. I remember feeling nervous, and I said four instead of five. The nurses started laughing, and when I looked to 12-year-old Isabel for help, I saw that she was laughing, too.

It may sound like a small thing to you, but given my history, that little incident hit me hard. I still remember the malicious laughter in vivid detail, and how I couldn't believe that my own sister was turning against me. That was the day I learned I was on my own.

I also began to understand Isabel's response to growing up in the same traumatic environment that I did. Unlike me,

Isabel did everything she could to fit in and be the shining star. She always had the right answer. She always did what was expected of her, intent on pleasing adults. She would get good grades in order to be trusted and admired. One summer, when she was only six years old, she won praise by reciting beautiful poems at a festival celebrating the Lady of the Serra. All the adults were in awe of her and she loved the attention. I believe she loved it so much that she falsified her true feelings just to be accepted.

As Alice Miller writes, "The real tragedy of people never given the chance to express their needs in childhood is that, without knowing it, they are leading a double life. ... They have constructed a false self in childhood and do not know that they have another one where their suppressed feelings and needs are hidden away as effectively as if under lock and key. The reason for this is that they have never encountered anyone who could help them understand their distress, identify the prison in which their feelings are confined, break out of that confinement, and articulate their true feelings and genuine needs."[8]

Isabel says that it was all the attention I received as a child — from being sick and problematic — that caused her to act that way. Whatever the reason, and despite the fact that her life seemed so easy to me, I remember feeling even as a little girl that Isabel was giving away an important piece her true self in order to gain approval. That just wasn't my way, and as a result I never really found my groove in Porto or anywhere else when I was around my family. I consistently got bad grades and felt out of step. I was always the under-performing student who screwed everything up. In fact, throughout my school years, I never had the impression that anyone ever believed in me.

---

[8] *The Truth Will Set You Free*, p. 73

After Elza and Laura finished their nursing internships, they rented an old house across the Douro River in Vila Nova de Gaia for the four of us. The city is known for the caves in which Port wine is aged. While our house was a modest dwelling, it was a symbol of success that my adult sisters lorded over me, along with their educations and their jobs. They both had superior attitudes that conflicted with my free spirit, and they repeatedly told me that I was the shame of the family. And Isabel, always trying to fit in, joined in the chorus by telling me that I was "the zero on the left." I simply didn't count.

By the tender age of nine I was already an outsider in my own family. The alienation I felt was really more traumatic than I could bear. I compensated by becoming very good at hiding my true feelings inside a tough exterior and by developing a highly sensitive bullshit meter. I also got good at preparing for emergencies and getting out of bad situations. Even to this day I make sure I always have money or credit cards on hand, and I always have an exit strategy when I'm in unfamiliar territory.

While these traits have served me well in various situations, I definitely paid a price for my independence — just as Isabel has paid a price for her compliance. What I didn't know was that by continuously repressing my true feelings of fear and anger I was setting myself up for years of suffering. During these difficult years I would constantly repeat my self-destructive habits and put up with malicious treatment from others. This compulsion to repeat my childhood trauma was my inner child's desperate attempt to get my attention, so that I could finally wake up and deal with the root cause of my various problems.

As Alice Miller puts it, children's brains are misled and their true emotions are banned. She theorized that the human brain is use-dependent; that it relies on experiences and environments to develop over the first four years of our existence. "The brain of a child who has mostly loving experiences will develop differently from the brain of a child who has been treated cruelly," she writes.[9] She goes on to say that because almost all children are beaten in the first years of their lives, their brain development is even more damaged.

While I wasn't spanked at home or scared of my father, my older sisters abused me emotionally and my teachers hit me all the time. My mother never called me names or forced things on me, like food I didn't like or her religious beliefs. Sadly my mother's only outlet to cope with her suffering was religion. This really harmed her by forcing her to have children she couldn't take care of or protect, just so the church could survive. It makes me so angry to realize how exploited she was! She used to pray alone all the time and would sometimes walk all the way to the chapel barefoot or on her knees, praying for a miracle. Of course, the miracle never came!

In spite of being contaminated by religion, my mother was actually a very intuitive and honest woman. When I asked her questions and she had no answer, she'd simply tell me that she didn't know instead of spreading some pretty little lie like my older sisters and teachers did. My mother wasn't educated, but she was wise and often showed me how much she cared. One time, a woman in the village asked her why she hadn't pierced my ears. "If she wants to have her ears pierced she can do it when she's an adult," my mother said. I loved this response because it gave me power.

Another time, when I was very little, I remember sleeping in my bed while my mother was outside taking care of the vegetable garden. She told my father to watch over me because my older brother Nuno was home from the mental

---

[9] "The Roots of Violence are NOT Unknown." Retrieved from: http://www.alice-miller.com/flyers_en.php

hospital and couldn't be trusted alone with little children. My father spaced out and left the house, and when my mother saw him outside she went up to him like a maniac and scolded him for leaving me alone with Nuno. I have no doubt that these experiences taught me that I was worth protecting and gave me courage throughout my life to stand up to those who were using me to fulfill their own needs.

I want to make clear that the abuse I suffered at the hands of my older sisters and teachers was a lot more harmful to me than the unavailability of my parents, although my parents' inability to really love and protect us was the catalyst. Just as Alice Miller writes, "This incapacity to love from the outset occurs much more often than we imagine. It is not the fault of the mothers but of the ignorance of society. In a progressive maternity ward a woman having her first baby should have access to enlightened assistance in perceiving and becoming fully aware of the body memories surfacing within her. This would prevent her from passing on traumas of her own childhood (abandonment, violence, and so on) to her baby."[10]

My parents' own repression resulted in their lack of emotional involvement, which made all of their children vulnerable to the abuse of others. One summer afternoon, when I was about five and my sister Isabel was about eight, we were walking home from the village and two teenagers scared us half to death by running after us and threatening to skin us alive. We were so scared when we got home that we couldn't talk about it! Even to this day, some people from the village continue to harass my family members and exploit their vulnerabilities, just for entertainment. It's sickening. But like Alice Miller says, "Sadism is not an infectious disease that strikes a person all of a sudden. It has long prehistory in

---

[10] *The Truth Will Set You Free*, p. 162

childhood..."[11] The oppression we all experienced outside the home no doubt had a dramatic effect on our brains and on our psyches.

"Studies on abandoned and severely mistreated Romanian children revealed striking lesions in certain areas of the brain and marked emotional and cognitive insufficiencies in later life," Alice Miller writes. "According to very recent neurobiological findings, repeated traumatization leads to an increased release of stress hormones that attack the sensitive tissue of the brain and destroy existing neurons. Other studies of mistreated children have revealed that the areas of the brain responsible for the 'management' of emotions are 20 to 30 percent smaller than in normal persons."[12]

Whatever traumas we undergo as children, Alice Miller believed that we have no choice but to suppress our anger against and our fear of the parents or other authority figures who humiliate us, kill our empathy and insult our dignity. We're simply not equipped emotionally to handle feelings that seem so starkly opposed to the people who, for better or for worse, are supporting our very existence. Instead of confronting the people responsible, we take out our rage later, as adults, on scapegoats. We mistreat our own children and spouses. We start fights and wars. And we even direct our anger against ourselves, with eating disorders, drug addiction, depression and, in my case, finding one bad relationship after another.

The traumatized child has a lot to deal with and nowhere to put it. In her first book, *The Drama of the Gifted Child*, Alice Miller writes that "it is precisely because a child's feelings are

---

[11] *For Your Own Good*, p. 265

[12] The Political Consequences of Child Abuse, *The Journal of Psychohistory* 26 (2) Fall 1998. Retrieved from: http://www.psychohistory.com/htm/06_politic.html

so strong that they cannot be repressed without serious consequences" later in life.[13] She begins that same book with her fundamental concept — one that I'll return to repeatedly — "that we have only one enduring weapon in our struggle against mental illness: the emotional discovery and emotional acceptance of the truth in the individual and the unique history of our childhood."[14]

The traumas I experienced in my early years, from the death of Zita and my severe dyslexia to my alienation from my family, were just precursors of the traumas I had yet to face and which I'll deal with in the following chapters. I'm a firm believer that the same is true for everyone who grows up in an imperfect world. While you may not have had the same traumatic experiences that I did, I'm willing to bet that you've had your share of things that upset you. We were all defenseless children once, and most of us were at the mercy of adults who were — to some degree — ignorant, incapable or downright vicious.

As human beings we can feel trauma in many ways. We can be beaten or neglected. We can be yelled at. We can be humiliated. But even things we don't often think of as traumas can have a negative impact on our future development. Being in an accident or living through a disaster like a hurricane or an earthquake, for example, can overwhelm a child.

In *The Untouched Key*, Alice Miller relates the story of how a three-year-old Pablo Picasso was affected by the tremendous earthquake that hit Malaga in 1884. His family fled their apartment and found shelter in a cave, where the

---

[13] *The Drama of the Gifted Child* (1994), p. 79
[14] Ibid., p. 26

young artist-to-be witnessed the birth of his sister in very scary circumstances. Fortunately, thanks to very supportive parents, Picasso was able to avoid becoming psychotic or criminal as a result of these traumas. As helping witnesses, Picasso's parents loved and protected him with empathy, compassion and hugs, so he could work out his traumas in more creative ways. Alice Miller looks at the famous painting *Guernica* as a glimpse inside the mind of Picasso as a child "while he was watching the dying people and horses and listening to the children screaming for help on the long walk to the shelter."[15]

Through people I've met I discovered another experience that can be extremely traumatic — being adopted. Even though it seems like such an act of love and sacrifice on the part of the adoptive parents, the complete and total rejection by the birth mother is difficult for many people to overcome. And quite often adoptive parents are too blinded by their own repression to see the real needs of the very traumatized children they bring into their lives. Many people adopt in order to fulfill their own desire to have children and not to help a traumatized child in need. Thus, they add to the child's trauma by projecting their own unresolved feelings onto their new son or daughter. No wonder adopted children are over-represented in prisons and mental health clinics worldwide!

Alice Miller holds out hope that any and all childhood traumas can be healed once and for all. Some just take longer than others. "We never know how a child will and must react to the injustice he or she has suffered," Alice Miller writes.[16]

---

[15] "The Childhood Trauma," excerpted from a lecture at New York's 92nd Street Y, October 22, 1998. Retrieved from: http://www.vachss.com/ guest_dispatches/alice_miller2.html

[16] *For Your Own Good*, p. 177

She believed that the timing of a trauma, the severity of it and the temperament of the victim all help determine how hard it will be for a person to work through.

While not everyone reacts to trauma in the same way, pretty much all of us experience it to some degree. And that's what makes Alice Miller so important. Hers is a solution that can help anyone, regardless of race, sex, class or cultural background. There's a comforting universality to Alice Miller's teachings. No matter what your personal history, there's no doubt in my mind that you can benefit from an honest exploration of the feelings of anger, fear, shame, guilt and frustration caused by your own childhood traumas.

Researchers are constantly learning more about the impact of trauma on children, while gaining a better understanding of how children sense the world around them. More and more caregivers are advocating more gentle infant deliveries, as well as the elimination of circumcisions and other mutilation rituals that are performed without any thought to the consequences their pain and trauma may cause.

Alice Miller believed that so many people are late to the party when it comes to avoiding the brutality of things like circumcision and spanking because they've been traumatized themselves. "The reason why parents mistreat their children has less to do with character and temperament than with the fact that they were mistreated themselves and were not permitted to defend themselves," she writes.[17] The vicious circle of trauma goes back countless generations.

Such systemic trauma can lead to the creation of monsters. If we all start out life as innocent little babies, why

---

[17] *For Your Own Good*, p. 105

do some of us turn out to be psychotic killers? Why are so many of us so self-destructive and insecure? Why do millions of people accept abusive relationships? Is it in the genes, or, as Alice Miller believed, the result of parental punishment and other traumas?

Dr. Bruce Perry, who directs the Child Trauma Academy in Houston, Texas, agrees with Alice Miller that violence begins in the brain as a result of traumatic experiences. "It's not the finger that pulls the trigger; it's the brain. It's not the penis that rapes; it's the brain," he says.[18] The organ that controls our behavior begins developing in the womb, and gets the bulk of its programming from our earliest relationships.

Robin Karr-Morse and David Lawrence Junior, who write about the importance of brain development in childhood, confirm Alice Miller's theories about the brain's use-dependence, which we already touched on earlier. "Experiences of all kinds literally stimulate electrical connections among brain cells as well as build gray matter in the brain," they write. "The stimulation a baby experiences before birth and in the first years of life shapes the type of brain the child develops. Those years are simply for developing capacities. An inadequate or traumatic caregiving relationship is deeply damaging, especially during those early years when the brain is forming chemically and structurally. That part of the brain that allows the baby to feel connected with another person can be lost or greatly impaired. Absent adequate nurturing by an emotionally competent caregiver, the baby faces an unpredictable tide of unregulated

---

[18] Quoted in *The Miami Herald*, "Violence and the Brain in Early Childhood Development," by Robin Karr-Morse and David Lawrence Jr., January 6, 2013. Retrieved from: http://www.miamiherald.com/2013/01/06/3168100/violence-and-the-brain-in-early.html

emotions. .... If a baby's experiences are pathological and steeped in chronic fear early in development, the very capacities that mitigate against violent behavior (including empathy, the capacity for self-regulation of strong emotions and the emotional modulation essential for complex problem-solving) can be lost. As these children grow into adolescence and adulthood, impulsive and aggressive behaviors are so often the outcomes. Moreover, genetic proclivities toward mental illness also are exacerbated. Communities inevitably absorb the consequences. We ignore the root of the problem at our peril."[19]

More and more medical professionals are confirming the theories put forward by Alice Miller from the late 1970s until her death in 2010. Dr. Gabor Maté, for example, confirms Alice Miller's contention that addiction, autism and other conditions aren't caused by genetics, but by trauma in childhood or even pre-birth in some cases. "The hardcore drug addicts that I treat ... are, without exception, people who have had extraordinarily difficult lives. And the commonality is childhood abuse," Dr. Maté says. "In other words, these people all enter life under extremely adverse circumstances. Not only did they not get what they needed for healthy development, they actually got negative circumstances of neglect. I don't have a single female patient in the Downtown Eastside who wasn't sexually abused, for example, as were many of the men, or abused, neglected and abandoned serially, over and over again. And that's what sets up the brain biology of addiction. In other words, the

---

[19] *The Miami Herald*, "Violence and the Brain in Early Childhood Development," by Robin Karr-Morse and David Lawrence Jr., January 6, 2013. Retrieved from: http://www.miamiherald.com/2013/01/06/3168100/violence-and-the-brain-in-early.html

addiction is related ... in terms of emotional pain relief and neurobiological development, to early adversity."[20]

Perhaps the largest single examination of childhood trauma comes in the form of the famous Adverse Childhood Experiences (ACE) study, conducted by the Centers for Disease Control and Prevention. The study incorporates responses from more than 17,000 participants. The initial phase of the landmark study was performed by Kaiser Permanente from 1995 to 1997 and demonstrated how specific childhood traumas can predict problems in adulthood. The baseline participants, who ranged in age from 19 to over 60 years old, are still being studied to determine their medical status.

Revealing the "staggering proof of the health, social and economic risks that result from childhood trauma," the study shows a significant link between a person's ACE score and their chances of being saddled with addictions and medical problems. Adults with an ACE score of 4, for example, were 460 percent more likely to have depression and 1,220 percent more likely to attempt suicide than adults with an ACE score of zero. The study concluded that a strong relationship exists "between the breadth of exposure to abuse or household dysfunction during childhood and multiple risk factors for several of the leading causes of death in adults."[21]

---

[20] "Dr. Gabor Maté on the Stress-Disease Connection, Addiction and the Destruction of American Childhood," December 25, 2012, Democracy Now! Retrieved from: http://www.democracynow.org/2012/12/25/dr_gabor_mat_on_the_stress

[21] ACE Study, cdc.gov/ace

ACE Study Traumatic Stressors

The adverse childhood experiences (ACEs) listed below were shown to have an impact on a person's health as an adult. As the number of ACEs increases, the risk for health problems increases in a strong and graded fashion. The percentages indicate the prevalence of each traumatic stressor in the original ACE study sample of 17,337 participants.

- Emotional Abuse   10.6%
- Physical Abuse   28.3%
- Sexual Abuse   20.7%
- Emotional Neglect   14.8%
- Physical Neglect   9.9%
- Mother Treated Violently   12.7%
- Household Substance Abuse   26.9%
- Household Mental Illness   19.4%
- Parental Separation or Divorce   23.3%
- Incarcerated Household Member   4.7%

Source: cdc.gov/ace

No wonder we're all so screwed up! Alice Miller puts it well when she says "the anger felt by every individual person stems from the primary, justified anger of the small child at the blows on it by the parents."[22] Think about what this means: When we're mad at our boyfriend, frustrated by a

---

[22] *Free From Lies*, p. 11

traffic jam or upset by our boss, we're on some level reenacting what happened to us as children.

It's also important to realize that unresolved trauma will always catch up with us. "Merely forgetting early traumas and early neglect is no solution," Alice Miller writes.[23] Instead, we have to go back in time and deal with the true feelings we had as children. Only then can we free ourselves from overwhelming fear, shame, guilt, anger and frustration.

Getting to that point is a lot easier when you have someone who can help you understand how present events trigger repressed feelings. Alice Miller calls the type of person who can help an adult face their childhood traumas an enlightened — or knowing — witness. Ideally, parents should fulfill the role of helping witnesses while their children are still little — like the young Pablo Picasso's parents did for their artist-to-be — but too many mothers and fathers are too traumatized themselves to provide the patience and loving support their children need. When most people grow up they unconsciously and compulsively reenact their own childhood traumas with people who have nothing to do with those painful scenarios, such as their own kids. Parents who have suffered are compelled to make sure that others suffer, too, and the cycle can go on for eternity.

Alice Miller broke that cycle of repression for me. But before I could become free I had to go through a lot of heartache. In the chapters that follow, I'll share stories from my past that illustrate the progression that can take people from their earliest traumas to ultimate freedom.

---

[23] *The Truth Will Set You Free*, p. 124

Worksheet: Recognize the Traumas from Your Childhood

Everyone has his or her own traumas, many of which can't even be remembered. For me, my sister Zita's burning isn't a memory I can recall. It happened and I was there, but my conscious mind has repressed it. The fact that other people have had to reproduce the memory for me makes it no less real or important to my personal history. Other traumas are a lot more obvious, like my emotionally unavailable father, my domineering sisters and my humiliating teachers, or even natural disasters like earthquakes and hurricanes.

1. List some of the traumas you may have experienced in your life, either directly or indirectly. Were you spanked as a child? Bullied by other children? Abused by an uncle? Try to run the gamut from seemingly minor incidents to major events.

2. In what ways, physically or emotionally, were your parents or other caregivers abusive to you when you were a child?

3. How did the people around you respond to your trauma when you were a child? Were you left to cope on your own? Were you told that spanking was good for you?

4. Alice Miller calls someone who can help another person clarify and understand his or her pain an enlightened witness. She also uses the term "helping witness" to describe someone who is kind to a child who's being misunderstood or mistreated. My mother's younger sister, who lived in Lisbon and often visited us, was truly

a helping witness for me when I was a child. She took time to explain things to me with kindness and patience, and was never mean to me. This can be extremely important for a child, and I try to fulfill this role with my own nieces and nephews. Was there anyone who was kind to you when you were a child, maybe a relative, teacher or neighbor who counterbalanced the cruelty that was otherwise dominant in your everyday life?

5. Because people unconsciously and compulsively reenact their childhood traumas in the present moment, your current circumstances can reveal a lot about what happened to you as a child. We often feel intense or overwhelming feelings when people or situations subconsciously remind us of painful childhood experiences. In these cases, it's important to connect your current problems to their root causes instead of the present-day triggers. What people or situations cause intense or overwhelming feelings in you today? How might these people or situations relate to your childhood experiences?

I was walking to my car one night after working at Bourbon Street, hot and sweaty from long hours of dancing. I smelled like an ashtray from all the second-hand smoke at the club. The clients were bad enough when it came to cigars and cigarettes back then, but the dancers were even worse. A lot of the girls would just hang out all night in the dressing room instead of working. And whenever I went in to freshen up or change my shoes quickly, I couldn't even see through the cloud of smoke. On that particular night, I was eager to just go home, wash the makeup off my face and veg out in front of the TV. But one of the dancers was celebrating her birthday and asked me to go with her and some of the other dancers for a drink. They had a limo waiting and were with a group of guys I didn't know. I politely told this girl that I needed to get home, but she insisted. "Come on, it's my birthday," she said. "Just have one drink with us and we'll bring you right back to your car." I was suspicious of the guys who were escorting her, but she assured me they were cool. Reluctantly, I agreed to go have a beer with them. As soon as I got into the limo and it drove out of the parking lot, I knew that one of the guys we were with was a time bomb ready to explode. My instincts told me that we weren't safe, and I planned to get out of the limo as soon it came to a stop. The birthday girl, Bianca, a pretty, fit, Spanish woman with a hot temper, was getting upset by this particular guy's chauvinistic attitude. Rather than just brush it off, she started pushing his buttons. I looked at her with my finger on my lips, trying to let her know that she should shut up unless she wanted to get slapped. She couldn't contain herself and I could feel that a fight was about to break out inside the limo. A few seconds later, the guy hit Bianca and she started hitting him back. I yelled to the driver to let me out, and before he even came to a complete stop I escaped without getting caught in the crossfire. I was pretty shaken up, so I called a taxi and went home for a quiet evening. That ride from hell was my first time in a limousine, and I don't have any desire to be in one again.

2. Fear

Traumatic experiences shake up our world and create feelings of fear, shame, anger, guilt and anxiety. As young children we don't really understand trauma, but we know that it doesn't feel good. We rely on our parents or other adults to protect us, and when they start adding to our pain we naturally become afraid.

Not so long after Isabel and I moved to Porto to be raised by my older sisters, my brother Amilcar — who was 20 years old and living in Spain — died in a car accident after leaving a party. It took a week for the body to get to Portugal, and it was a difficult time for my family. It was like time stood still forever. As with Zita's death by fire, no one talked about the accident because it was just too frightening. The unspoken rule in our family was that we couldn't say anything about any of the children who passed.

I found out after the funeral that my brother died at the scene of the accident, even though my older sisters told me differently. I was mad at them for lying to me because I actually prayed really hard for God to save my brother, thinking he had a fighting chance in a hospital somewhere. I didn't believe much in God but I prayed anyway, and it pissed me off that my sisters thought they had to make up some story to make me feel better. My sisters have lied about virtually everything all their lives and justified that behavior under the guise of protecting others against painful truths. They didn't realize that while truth might hurt temporarily, lies prevent healing. Lies hurt forever.

Amilcar's death marked the beginning of a very troubled time for me. The collected traumas of my illnesses, my learning disability and our painful family dynamics were getting the best of me.

My anxieties had the side effect of making me too much to handle for Elza and Laura. My two sisters enjoyed their easy dominance over Isabel, but I was a different breed. My lack of compliance annoyed my sisters to no end. The more I fought back, the more they were determined to rein me in.

My sister Elza was a great manipulator. She played the role of the "mother" in our household and used all forms of seduction to get us to do things. Everyone in our family circle, and many outside it, thought she was so wonderful for always helping others, both in her professional life as a nurse and in her personal life as well.

I learned later on that Elza's helpfulness was a strategy to keep her distracted from her own traumas and fears. I think she means well, but she feels a tremendous amount of guilt and responsibility for actions that enabled the compulsions of her younger siblings, especially Laura and Isabel. These feelings blind her and drive her to try to fix things, but the more she gets involved, the more compulsions she fuels and the more guilt she feels. Guilt protects her from feeling the raw pain of her own childhood and keeps her — and those around her — trapped in a vicious circle of compulsive repetition. "Every patient clings to fantasies in which he sees himself in the active role so as to escape the pain of being defenseless and helpless," Alice Miller writes. "To achieve this he will accept guilt feelings, although they bind him to neurosis."[24]

You see, when Elza was born my mother was only 17 and didn't know anything about raising kids. My mother was still a child herself. Elza was a beautiful baby, and my mother saw her as a pretty little doll to play with. The contrast between the way my mother treated Elza and the way she treated Laura was pretty big. Elza was showered with attention and kisses, but Laura became the family maid. My mother asked Elza to cook and clean, but she never could do it the right way and Laura was much more organized and obedient. By age 10, Laura was doing all the chores around the house and even cooking breakfast for my father and the other men who worked on the roads near the village. Elza had more opportunities to do whatever she wanted and she usually spent her free time reading books.

Elza always had a strange mix of guilt and admiration when it came to Laura. Elza felt bad that Laura had to do all the dirty work, and she looked up to Laura for being able to follow the rules. Laura could have easily resented Elza, but Elza did everything she could to make up for her inability to cook and clean by supporting Laura's dreams of building a career and having a family.

As a result, Elza and Laura became very close. Elza's guilt and Laura's anger gave them a common enemy in our mother and they took every opportunity to lash out. Elza was particularly harsh and I remember feeling so sorry for my mother when they made her cry. It was usually about stupid stuff, like how to do the dishes correctly, and I just didn't get it at the time. Today I understand that Elza and Laura were unconsciously punishing my mother for bringing them into the world and not meeting their needs when they were little.

---

[24] *Banished Knowledge*, p. 74

My sisters unconsciously made my mother — and others — pay for their miserable childhoods. It's not surprising that my sisters are pro-lifers. By being in the healthcare profession, they've counseled many women to have children they didn't want, instead of guiding them to have the abortions they needed. Unconsciously, my sisters want others to be born to suffer and have the same fate as they did. If they had found out about my pregnancy when I was 20, they would have forced me to carry it to term and give birth to a new being — just so they could hate me for having a child in the same way they hated my mother for having all of us. They'd have another scapegoat on which to take out their repression, which is absolute insanity!

Elza's desperate efforts to remedy past mistakes by trying to make things perfect worked easily with Isabel, who was rewarded for complying and became the family favorite hands down. But I saw right through the bullshit. I tried to please Elza at first, but no matter how hard I tried it was never good enough. She always made me do the same things over and over again to keep me busy, just so she wouldn't have to worry about me causing more embarrassment to the family.

For example, Elza used my difficulties at school to keep me in line. She used to teach in the village, so she took it upon herself to help me do better in school. This might have been nice, but she didn't know how to work with my dyslexia any better than my real teachers did. It was just awful. She kept a big blackboard in the kitchen, where she made me practice endless spelling and math lessons. If I didn't do something right, I'd have to keep doing it. I was spending so much time in Elza's "classroom" that I had no time to even look at my real schoolwork!

Maybe Elza believed that she was doing these things for my own good, but she was really just making up for her own guilt at getting to skate through life when she was young. It seemed as if my being happy was a sign of trouble to Elza, a trigger of her own fears, shame and guilt. So the only way I could have any fun was to sneak out of the house whenever I had the chance. Escaping was so hard that if I managed it I wouldn't come home until I was exhausted and starving. Elza would usually be waiting up for me, ready to yell at me for being so irresponsible.

When her psychological manipulations didn't work, Elza looked to Laura for help controlling me. Laura made up for her own childhood traumas by playing the "father" role in our household. She worked all the time, day and night. Making money was the driving force in her life, and she was desperate to get married and have children so she could boss more people around.

True to form, Laura ended up marrying a guy who had intense social phobias. He was incredibly shy and very easy for her to dominate. For a while we all lived in the same house, and he would spend most of his time locked in his room. Whenever he needed to go out, we all had to make ourselves scarce. Years later he grew to like me, and until the day he died I was the only one in our family he could trust. When I used to visit Portugal in the summer as an adult, he would come out of his room just to say hello to me.

Laura's "father" role extended to our parents, too. Just before Laura got married, my parents visited us in Porto and Laura had my father committed to a mental hospital. He never forgave her for putting him there against his will. She said that she was only trying to help him get treatment for his drinking problem, but I believe she was using her medical connections to hide our father's alcoholism from her husband-to-be.

While Elza played her mind games with me, Laura was the one who would use physical force. She'd do things like stand in the doorway so I couldn't get out of the house. And between the two of them, my sisters did everything they could to make my life a living hell. They screamed and yelled. They made threats. They followed me to the café where I met my friends and shamed me in front of them. To add to my embarrassment, they yelled at my friends for being a bad influence on me. They even resorted to medication, but after the first time they did it I just pretended to take the pills they gave me.

One sunny, summer weekend I had plans to meet a few friends at the local café before we all went to the beach. Secretly, Elza wanted me to stay home. She acted very nice for once, and even offered to give me a vitamin injection to help me feel more alert. I watched her take the syringe out of the vitamin box, but she must have switched it for a very strong narcotic. In a matter of minutes, as I was going to meet my friends, I got weak in the knees and could barely walk. I was swerving all over the place and could have been hit by a car! Instead of going to the beach I stayed in bed at a friend's house all day, and I learned never to take "vitamins" from my sisters ever again.

Elza and Laura also tried to lock me up in our fourth-floor apartment, but that didn't work either. One time, I jumped from one patio to the next until I found an open door to go through. I was the star of my own action movie! My sisters decided they didn't want to come home one day to find me splattered on the ground, so they never pulled that stunt again.

While I remained defiant, underneath it all I was incredibly scared. I lived in constant fear of my sisters and their spying, controlling ways. I had to always be on my guard. I desperately wanted their love and approval like Isabel was getting, but I knew I would never get it on my own terms.

Things got so bad that Elza finally told me she never wanted to see me again. So at age 11, I ran away for the first time and made a train station my new home. I hid in the public bathrooms for about a week until the police found me and took me in. They looked to see if I matched any of the photos of reported runaways. My picture was in their book, but I hadn't slept much and was such a mess that they didn't even recognize me. The officers talked rough to me. I kept my mouth shut because I never cooperated with anyone unless they spoke with kindness, no matter how scared I was of what they might do to me. I was a rebel with a cause. So it wasn't until a new, gentler officer arrived that I opened up and agreed to let the police call my family.

When I returned home my sisters seemed relieved to see me again. They no doubt felt like they would've gotten in trouble if anything really bad had happened to me. Elza started acting really nice, and I have to admit that the illusion of her love was comforting. But it didn't last very long. Soon we were butting heads again and driving each other crazy.

Alice Miller explains that most of us aren't capable of genuine feelings, and that most relationships are held together by fear and guilt. "We cannot really love if we are forbidden to know our truth, the truth about our parents and caregivers as well as about ourselves," she writes. "We can only try to behave as if we were loving, but this hypocritical behavior is the opposite of love. It is confusing and deceptive, and it produces much helpless rage in the deceived person. This rage must be repressed in the presence of the pretended 'love,' especially if one is dependent, as a child is, on the person who is masquerading in this illusion of love."[25]

Elza's illusion of kindness definitely helped to further repress the rage I was feeling inside. My feelings of fear and anger would bubble up when she began to mistreat me again, but then she'd feel guilty and act nice for a while. What a rollercoaster ride! I wanted so desperately to believe in her love, but knowing that it could end at any time kept me in a constant state of fear.

During my tween and teenage years, larger forces that weighed on my psyche were also at work. On April 25, 1974, a *coup d'état* threw out the ailing Salazar, replacing his fascist regime with a democratic one. At the time, though, no one could say what was happening or where the new leaders would take the country. At school, the result was daily mayhem. Teachers felt less secure than ever, and classrooms became unruly, even chaotic. Learning was even harder for me than it was before and very quickly it became too much for me, so I dropped out at age 15 when I found out that I wasn't going to pass seventh grade.

Without school I found myself even more at the mercy of my sisters. They insisted that I get a job to keep busy, but everything they found for me required working all day for little or no pay. They wanted to keep me occupied and out of trouble, with little chance of having any money I could use to go out and have a good time.

This was really nothing new because Elza and Laura had done the same thing to ruin my summer vacations when I was in school. One time, when I was only 14, they sent me to a miserable live-in job at a private hospital run by nuns. I had to clean the place from 7:00 a.m. until late at night — without

---

[25] *The Drama of the Gifted Child* (1994), p. 66

pay. I hated it, and I hated my sisters for sending me there so they wouldn't have to worry about me.

It wasn't long before I ran away again. I did so repeatedly, but I could never seem to get far enough away. And besides, my problems kept following me wherever I went.

With an oppressive home life and not much luck in school or at my various slave jobs, I felt so alone that I started fantasizing about suicide. But with a little luck and a lot of hard looking, I finally found paying work in a hospital taking care of newborn babies. I was assigned the night shift, and I genuinely loved watching after those young, helpless and innocent souls. For the first time I could really remember, I was happy. I was earning pretty good money for a 15-year-old, and I even had time to go out on my nights off.

One night I was called to help in the delivery room and for the first time ever I saw a baby being born. It was quite a scene. The woman was doing it naturally without painkillers. She cursed out her husband and threw the IV across the room. I tried to pick everything up and hold the woman down. Then the baby got stuck just as it was crowning. The doctor used a sucking machine that pulled really hard on the baby's head. Then he asked for scissors to cut the woman open. When he noticed the horror on my face as I watched him tear open her flesh, he told me not to worry. "She's not feeling me cutting her, she's in too much pain from the labor," he said nonchalantly. I felt like throwing up.

Finally, the baby came out and was whisked off to a machine that would help it breathe. In its first 30 minutes the only thing that little baby experienced was trauma! The baby was going to be "fine," they all said, but I made up my mind right then and there that I'd never bring a child into this screwed up world.

Having children was never something I was interested in. Even as a young girl I remember thinking about how mean the adults in my village were to their children and animals. If I were the mother of one of those mean people, I just couldn't live with myself. I wouldn't want to be a mother unless I knew for sure that I could give birth to a loving human being. Today, thanks to Alice Miller's writings, I know I could raise a child to be a healthy, happy adult. And if I ever find myself pregnant in a loving relationship and we both want the baby, I'd carry the pregnancy to term and not be afraid. The chances of that ever happening are pretty slim, if not impossible. I've never met a man who's liberated himself, and I would never have a child with a man who still lives with — and believes in — lies and illusions. I don't have any expectations that I'll ever meet a truly liberated man, but my door is always open.

In addition to cementing my determination not to have children, my job at the hospital was good for me in other, more immediate ways. For the first time in my life I had my own money, so I didn't need to rely on my sisters or resort to taking change from their wallets like I used to. Before I started working at the hospital, petty theft was my only recourse. Elza and Laura made it clear that they'd never give me anything because I was a "bad girl." Isabel on the other hand, "the good girl," got everything from them. With my first paycheck I bought a pair of bright red short shorts. I felt so sexy in them, and being able to buy them for myself gave me a sense of power I had never before experienced.

On my nights off from work I'd hang out with my friends in cafés. We'd usually talk about how screwed up the adults in our lives were. We pretended to be cool, but all of us were searching for answers, just trying to figure it all out without admitting out loud how frightened we were. We weren't just scared of our parents and authority. We were also scared of what the future held.

We didn't drink much, maybe a beer here and there. That was really it. We pretty much stuck to soft drinks, water, coffee and tea while we smoked cigarettes and ranted on about life as a teenager. We laughed at all the things our families thought we were up to. They had wild imaginations! We usually just stayed up late listening to Pink Floyd and Frank Zappa music. I'd show up at home at about 7:00 a.m. and go right to sleep, pretending I was just coming back from work.

I was usually the only girl in a group of about four or five boys who liked to hang out. I always had more fun being one of the boys. I liked to play football and ride bikes, and I wore pants instead of skirts and dresses. My male friends all thought it was cool and treated me as an equal.

Eventually, I developed a huge crush on one of the boys. It was the same year I started developing breasts, which just kept on growing! I hated having big breasts when I was trying to fit in with the guys and I did everything I could to hide them. But I couldn't hide my feelings for Jorge. I thought he was beautiful, inside and out. I always sat next to him, laughed at his jokes and tried to spend time with him every chance I got. The first time I put a dress on I was probably trying to get Jorge's attention. But he never tried anything and neither did I. We were still more like kids than adults, and we really weren't sure about anything yet.

The independence I got from my job at the hospital and the validation I got from my male peers made me so happy that my sisters got suspicious. To them, my happiness could only mean that I was up to no good. They had me on their radar and were looking for clues to find out what was going on.

One night — or so the story goes — my supervisor at the hospital called the house to see if I could come in on my day off. As usual, I had told my sisters that I was going to work that night and was already out with my friends. Remember, these were days without cell phones!

The next morning when I arrived home my sisters laid into me like you wouldn't believe. They demanded to know where I was the night before, what I was doing and with whom I was doing it. I ran into the bathroom and locked myself in. My sisters banged on the door until they had to go to work.

Later that day my sister Laura told me that I needed a strong hand to keep me in line. She had already tried to assume the father role in our household and I figured that rant of hers was just another way of threatening me. I really didn't think much of it, and just assumed that things would blow over before too long.

A few days later my brother Eliseu showed up out of the blue. I thought he just came by for a visit, but I eventually learned that Elza and Laura had asked him to come over to take me to Spain against my will. They told him that they couldn't control me and that I needed a man's discipline to get in line.

Eliseu announced that he was going to visit our parents and he asked me if I'd like to go along. I told him that I'd like to go, but that I had to work and wouldn't have a couple of nights off for a few days. He said he'd wait for me, and I asked him how long he planned to stay with our folks. He assured me that it would just be a quick trip and that he'd bring me back home in time for work. So I agreed to go with him, and we spent some time in our old village.

It was actually nice to see my mother and father. We all had a relaxed and happy visit, and I was glad to get a break from Elza and Laura. But when we were supposed to start heading back to Porto, my brother didn't seem to be in any hurry to leave. I was afraid I'd get in trouble at work, so I begged him to get moving. When we finally got in the car, Eliseu took a totally different direction. I was in a near panic, not knowing what was going on. He said that he needed to talk to me. Alone.

He kept driving and I kept getting more nervous. Finally we stopped in the middle of nowhere and Eliseu explained that we weren't going back to Porto at all. My life there was over because of all my bad behavior, he told me, and I should just learn to accept it. He said that he was taking me to Spain where he could make sure I didn't cause any more trouble for myself or for our family.

Of course I started crying hysterically, accusing Eliseu and my sisters of destroying my life. My job and my independence meant everything to me. How dare they try to take it away!

We drove back to my parents' house to spend one more night there before leaving for Spain. When everyone was asleep, I left the house and started making the 125-mile journey back to Porto on foot. Every time a car or truck went by, I put my thumb out. Plenty of truck drivers were willing to give a lift to a pretty 15-year-old with big breasts who was walking all alone in the middle of the night!

The drivers didn't ask any questions, but most of them tried to touch me. I was usually able to talk them out of it. I'd simply ask them if they wanted their sisters or other women in their lives to be treated with respect. The strategy didn't work so well with the last driver, however. It was about 4:00 or 5:00 in the morning and we were just outside the Porto city limits. When I wouldn't give in willingly to his advances, he hit me and then he tried to rape me. I screamed that he'd have to kill me first. Then I started hitting myself really hard. He got so freaked out that he opened the door and pushed me out. Luckily, I was close enough to home that I could take public transportation the rest of the way.

I made sure I got home when my sisters were all at work so I wouldn't have to confront them right away. I got some rest, cleaned up and left the house before they returned home. But when I showed up for work at the hospital later that evening I got some bad news. My supervisor told me that my family had been in contact with her, revealing that I was under age and couldn't work there anymore without their permission. I begged the people at the hospital to let me stay on, but they said there was nothing they could do.

I left, devastated. And as I sat on the sidewalk in front of the Hospital do Terço, with its beautiful blue and white tiled façade, Eliseu pulled up foaming at the mouth. He screamed at me to get in the car. I had nowhere to turn so I went along with him, headed for who knew what in Spain.

When we got to La Coronada, a small village in the province of Badajoz where Eliseu worked as a heavy equipment operator, I have to say that it was nice to see my four-year-old niece and three-year-old nephew. They were so adorable! And for a while, despite being uprooted, life in Spain wasn't so bad. Loli, my sister-in-law, convinced Eliseu to let me go out on my own now and then, and she introduced me to some of the local girls.

The youth there would meet every night in the local bar and then walk up and down the main road. That's how I met Justino, the first boy I ever kissed. We started spending a lot of time together and soon found a tree to sit under so we could talk and make out all night long. It was all pretty innocent, but someone told my brother that I was fooling around with the doctor's son. Eliseu naturally freaked out and decided that locking me in my room was the perfect solution to the problem. The room had bars on the windows and I wasn't allowed out except to have meals with the family and to go to the bathroom.

For a while, Justino sent his six-year-old brother to deliver notes to me. But getting a few love notes in prison was no substitute for freedom. After one more brief shot at happiness, I was completely hopeless again. I couldn't see a way out. So, alone in my room, I took out a bottle filled with all the pills my sisters had tried to give me in Porto and swallowed them all in a desperate attempt to put myself out of my misery. I slipped into unconsciousness and finally released myself.

My sister-in-law found me several hours later when it was time for dinner. I was slumped lifeless on the floor like some discarded rag doll. In a panic, Loli rushed me to the hospital where a team of doctors worked frantically to save me. I spent a few days in a coma, and when I finally woke up I got mad because my plan had failed. I kept pulling out my IV in the hopes that I'd die right there in the hospital. The last thing I wanted to do was go back to Eliseu, my latest oppressor!

Because I was in the hospital as a result of a suicide attempt, the authorities were on their way to interview me. But since I was also in Spain illegally without a passport, my brother got scared and took me out of the hospital without permission. I was still drugged up when Eliseu and Loli drove me back to my parents' house in Portugal, a two-day drive. I pretty much slept the whole time. It actually took me a few months to get back to normal.

I faced a lot of harmful treatment throughout my teenage years that kept me on edge all the time. It may be true that my sisters were trying to help me, but their misguided efforts had a damaging effect. If I had had a different temperament I might have really believed that I wasn't any good and was simply undeserving of anything better than I got. In my dancing days, I saw way too many women who were so beaten down emotionally that they had no self-respect at all. For some reason I never stopped believing in myself, even when no one else believed in me. I was confused, angry and scared, but on some level, the core belief that I was better than my oppressors kept me alive.

Alice Miller once said, "pain is the way to the truth. By denying that you were unloved as a child you spare yourself some pain, but you are not with your own truth."[26] Because we're so scared of not getting love, we avoid this healing pain and end up repeating our traumas over and over again. "Nobody can confront being neglected or hated without feeling guilty," Alice Miller went on to say in the same interview. We create this false guilt because we're so terrified of the realization that our parents — or anyone else we looked up to — didn't love us. Feeling guilty about our own perceived responsibility for what others have done to us may protect us from facing our fears, but it actually does much more damage: It supports our blindness and keeps us shackled in the chains of repetition compulsion.

As I tried to grow up through my late teens and early twenties, my descent into guilt, blindness and neurosis was only just beginning. I was, at times, afraid that my siblings were right about me and that I'd never amount to much. Deep down I believed in myself, but my family members were relentless in their ability to tell me what a screw-up I was.

It only occurred to me after reading Alice Miller that my family was also scared of me. I was a threat to them because I came close to shattering their own illusions. The only choice they had was to try and control me so they could avoid their own pain — the pain they feared the most.

---

[26] *Free from Lies*, p. 202–203

Worksheet: Uncover Your Trauma-Related Fears

When we experience trauma as children, especially physical abuse at the hands of our own parents, deep down we know that something is wrong and it makes us afraid. But since facing our fears is impossible as children, our only recourse is repression and denial. To defend our parents we often try to find ways to blame ourselves for the mistreatment we receive.

1. Think back to your childhood and reflect on how the traumas you experienced made you feel.

2. What were you scared of as a child or a teenager? Were you able to talk to anyone about your fears? Did you have any "helping witnesses" who listened to you and treated you with respect?

3. How do you keep repressing intense feelings when they start to surface? Do you turn to things like yoga, meditation, food, alcohol, relationships or medication? Do you strive for success? What other techniques are you using now to avoid facing your childhood fears?

When people threw bachelor parties at Bourbon Street, the guys who were getting married would usually go up on stage and make complete fools of themselves. The dancers would make the guys walk on all fours like dogs and spank them on their butts — sometimes really hard and with a belt. Some girls enjoyed taking advantage of the situation and showed no mercy! I always refused to get involved. I never understood why any man would ever subject himself to this kind of treatment. After reading Alice Miller, I came to understand that people who were spanked as children on a regular basis repeated their childhood trauma by acting out with rough sex — and getting beat up by topless dancers.

3. Repression

Alice Miller often talks about the "life-saving function of repression."[27] As defenseless little children we have no choice but to subconsciously repress our negative feelings for two reasons. First of all, we need support from others. And second, we just don't have the ability to understand how the people we must rely on could actually be cruel to us. In the short-term, repression can have a positive effect in traumatic circumstances.

But the subconscious actions that we think are saving our life as children are what really keep us down as adults. In fact, Alice Miller believed that it wasn't so much the traumas we experience that harm us, but "the unconscious, repressed, hopeless despair over not being allowed to give expression to what one has suffered and the fact that one is not allowed to

---

[27] *Breaking Down the Wall of Silence*, p. 110

show and is unable to experience feelings of rage, anger, humiliation, despair, helplessness and sadness."[28]

Abused and otherwise traumatized children are forced to repress their true feelings, unless they're lucky enough to find someone to comfort them. But because enlightened witnesses (and even helping witnesses) aren't always readily available, most of us develop what Alice Miller calls a false self — usually for the sake of our parents — only to pay for it later in life.

In an article entitled "The Essential Role of an Enlightened Witness in Society," Alice Miller writes that "it seems clear to me that information about abuse inflicted during childhood is recorded in our body cells as a sort of memory, linked to repressed anxiety. If, lacking the aid of an enlightened witness, these memories fail to break through to consciousness, they often compel the person to violent acts that reproduce the abuse suffered in childhood, which was repressed in order to survive. The aim is to avoid the fear of powerlessness before a cruel adult. This fear can be eluded momentarily by creating situations in which one plays the active role, the role of the powerful, towards a powerless person."[29]

This is how the vicious cycle of parental abuse continues for generations. And in extreme cases, the repetition compulsion can lead to violent atrocities against humanity. "To his dying day, Hitler was convinced that only the death of every single Jew could shield him from the fearful and daily memory of his brutal father," Alice Miller writes. "Since his father was half Jewish, the whole Jewish people had to be exterminated. I know how easy it is to dismiss this interpretation of the Holocaust, but I honestly haven't yet

---

[28] *For Your Own Good*, p. 259

[29] "The Essential Role of an Enlightened Witness in Society," retrieved from: http://www.alice-miller.com/articles_en.php?lang=en&nid=41&grp=11

found a better one. Besides, the case of Hitler shows that hatred and fear cannot be resolved through power, even absolute power, as long as the hatred is transferred to scapegoats. On the contrary, if the true cause of the hatred is identified, is experienced with the feelings that accompany this recognition, blind hatred of innocent victims can be dispelled. ... Old wounds can be healed if exposed to the light of day. But they cannot be repudiated by revenge."[30]

In milder cases, which cover the majority of human beings on this planet, our repression tricks us into believing in the false self until we die with our lies or until something like depression, psychoses or physical illness jars us out of our illusion. The tragedy of our existence is that most of us aren't even aware of the fact — or find out too late — that we've lost all love and respect for who we really are. Repression is an evil that prevents many people from even giving Alice Miller's theories a second look, because they seem so radical to someone who's totally repressed.

The fact that repression hides our truth is why writing this book is so important for me. Because I know how great it feels to be free from lies and illusions, I want to make the experience possible for as many people as I can. Great forces were at work against me, but I'm here to tell you that they can all be overcome. It may take a lot of courage, and it may force you to see your childhood with new eyes, but the personal liberation is worth any pain you need to go through to get there.

After I tried to kill myself while under the care of my brother Eliseu — but before I found myself back in Portugal

---

[30] "The Essential Role of an Enlightened Witness in Society," retrieved from: http://www.alice-miller.com/articles_en.php?lang=en&nid=41&grp=11

with Elza and Laura — I had another misadventure in Spain. I agreed to help my brother Carlos and his wife take care of their kids and I ended up being treated like a slave for three months.

Carlos lived in a small village close to Oviedo, in the province of Asturias. My life had gotten somewhat back to normal since I had the chance to rest and recover at my parents' house, and when I was feeling strong again I went to visit Carlos with my mother. It was just a short taxi ride from our village in Portugal. We had a nice time and when my mother decided it was time to go, my brother and his wife asked me if I wanted to stay for a few months to help out with their new baby.

I admired my brother Carlos, so I agreed to stay. I thought he was the coolest. He kind of looks like Charlie Sheen — who I would meet 16 years later at Bourbon Street — and I soon found out that he was just as crazy! I had no idea how neurotic he really was until I started living with him and his family. One time, I made soup for dinner and he screamed at me for serving it to him when it was too hot. He yelled so loud that he scared his children half to death, and I remember wondering why he hated me so much.

My sister-in-law Sabina was just as pleasant. She fought with Carlos all the time and she treated me like her servant. For some reason, I was the only person who could stop the new baby from crying. The little guy was only content if I was carrying him. When he fell asleep in my arms I'd try to put him down in his bed very carefully so I could just hang out in my room and relax for a little bit, but as soon as I put him down he'd wake up and start crying again. My sister-in-law would come racing in, yelling at me to hold the baby. It was exhausting.

The stress of being in Carlos' house was the last thing I needed. I can't remember exactly how long I was there, but I missed my period the whole time because of the anxiety. I finally stood up to my brother and demanded that he take me back to Portugal. During one of our many fights over this particular topic, he threw me on my bed and punched a big hole in the door. But I refused to back down. And finally, after several weeks, Carlos had enough of me. One weekend he put me in the car and took me back to our parents' house. While I was relieved to be out of his house, I soon found myself back in Vila Nova de Gaia with Elza and Laura.

had just turned 17 and my sisters thought they had finally found someone who could tame me. His name was Dr. Julio Machado Vaz. At the time he was young and unknown, but today he's Portugal's most famous sexologist. He has several best-selling books and a TV show that's a lot like Dr. Phil's.

To get so popular all Julio talked about was sex. Sex was his obsession, and he got all of Portugal to enable his addiction. He became a high-profile celebrity advisor. But before he hit the big time, his methods were unprofessional to say the least. From my personal experience, he was extremely abusive.

My sister Laura worked at the public clinic where Julio was building his reputation. Back then he was a dashing 27-year-old doctor. His mother, Maria Clara, was a famous singer, and his father, Julio Machado Vaz de Sousa, was a respected faculty member at the University of Porto's medical school. Given Laura's connections, it was easy for me to get an appointment to see this rising young star. And he was more than willing to take me on as a patient.

When we met, the first question he asked me was whether or not I had a boyfriend. When I said no, he asked if I'd ever had one. Once again, I said no. Then he told me that my sister brought me to see him because she was afraid that I was sexually active. He explained to me that sex is normal, that most people are sexually repressed and that what I needed was a boyfriend.

After just one visit in the clinic he moved our sessions to his private office. He pressed his advantage and manipulated me into having oral sex with him. I knew he was just using me and that he didn't have a clue about how to really help me, but I kept seeing him to spite Laura and the others. Our little arrangement went on for months, and the whole time I was thinking, "What would my sisters think of their charming doctor now, the one man they thought could solve all my problems?"

Looking back I almost can't believe how despicable this so-called doctor was. One time, he took me to his house while his wife was at the hospital having his second baby. Obviously, part of me was aware that what we were doing was wrong, but I was so focused on somehow harming my sisters that I let him get away with it.

When he was tired of his latest conquest, Julio ended our sessions. I imagine that he found another patient to fool around with. In an interview many years later a reporter asked him, "Is a psychiatrist also a seducer?"

"Maybe the reverse is more true," was my doctor's smug response.[31]

Such a reply should have exposed him. But people in Portugal, and everywhere else in the world for that matter, are too emotionally blind to recognize even the most obvious red flags. Julio revealed just how sick he really was, but by then he was all but glorified for being an outlet for the whole country's sexual repression. The people of Portugal still live

---

[31] Teixeira da Silva, Helena, *Noticias*, 8-25-07. Retrieved 2013 from: http://entre-vidas.blogspot.com/2007/09/jlio-machado-vaz.html

vicariously through the escapades of this bold doctor who talks so openly about sex. And no doubt he continues to take full advantage of the collective repression for his own pleasure. In my opinion, it's absolutely disgraceful.

Interestingly, Alice Miller has a few words to say about the seduction dramas that are reenacted by men like Julio who are compelled to use women. "The seducer is loved, admired, and sought after by many women because his attitude awakens their hopes and expectations," she writes. "They hope that their need for mirroring, echoing, respect, attention and mutual understanding, which has been stored up inside them since early childhood, will finally be fulfilled by this man. But these women not only love the seducer, they also hate him, for he turns out to ... be unable to fulfill their needs and soon abandons them. They feel hurt by the demeaning way he treats them because they cannot understand him. Indeed, he does not understand himself."[32]

All I really knew at the time was that I was more confused than ever. Dr. Julio Machado Vaz's "treatment" made me a lot worse off. And my sexual encounters with him opened the door to exactly what my sisters feared most. What's more, the abuse I suffered at the hands of this doctor was harmful to my sister Isabel. If he had given me the help I really needed, I would have given better advice to my sister five years later.

When Isabel broke up with her boyfriend of 10 years and started feeling some of her own repressed childhood feelings, I did exactly what Julio did to me. Instead of giving her emotional support and helping her use her pain to set herself free, I encouraged her to sleep around. I "treated" my sister with sex by introducing her to other guys, hoping she would forget about her boyfriend. This only made her repress her

---

[32] *Thou Shalt Not Be Aware*, p. 80

true self once again, and I believe it contributed to her ultimate downfall.

The chain of harm done by doctors, therapists and gurus under the guise of help is endless. Alice Miller believed that most people with a "Dr." in front of their name or a "Ph.D." at the end of it weren't in any kind of position to help or guide anyone, especially if they were repressing their own traumas and creating their own illusions. For many years I blamed myself for what happened with Dr. Julio Machado Vaz. It took me more than two decades to see the truth and speak about the fact that this doctor had exploited my anger at my family to feed his sexual perversions and abuse me sexually, instead of helping me work through and resolve my anger.

In the book *Boundaries: Where You End And I Begin*, Anne Katherine states, "A therapist is entrusted with his or her clients' deepest secrets. A minister bestows sanctions from the highest power in the universe. The potential for harm is overwhelming. For a person in such a role, essentially that of a guardian, to cross sexual boundaries is a grave violation. A child, a client, a patient, a follower or a worshiper are vulnerable and usually approach authority out of need. A sexual action by a guardian is very confusing, even to a very strong and healthy individual. For someone vulnerable and in need, such an action can be devastating. When a parent is sexual toward a child, the violation reverberates for decades. Trust is broken, the child takes on responsibility for the act, sexuality is affected, and the bond is damaged. When a therapist, physician, attorney or clergy person is sexual with a client or worshiper, it is also incest. A trust is broken, a bond is perverted. The person who sought care was used to meet the needs of the caregiver."[33]

---

[33] Katherine, Anne. *Boundaries: Where You End and I Begin*, p. 87–88

I didn't need sex or a boyfriend when I saw Dr. Julio Machado Vaz. What I needed was an enlightened witness to help me feel my repressed pain and give me a better way to deal with my self-righteous, overbearing, domineering, invasive and authoritarian sisters and brothers.

After going for "counseling," my repressed anger — at my sisters for thinking the worst; at Dr. Julio Machado Vaz for sexualizing me before the time was right and for not teaching me how to protect myself against pregnancy by giving me birth control pills; and even at my parents for bringing me into this world when they were in no position to protect me — fueled my sexual appetite. For a while, if a sexy guy approached me I wouldn't miss the opportunity to sleep with him. If this was what everybody in my family was thinking about me anyway, I decided to just go ahead and do it.

I was actually pretty picky and said "no" more often than not. You'd be surprised how many Portuguese men don't understand what that word means, but I made it pretty clear to the guys I wasn't interested in. I was happy to go for months without sex if no one special was around, but if I thought someone was attractive, friendly, smart and fun I'd give in to the pleasure of the moment.

At the age of 20 I found myself pregnant. I knew I couldn't bring a new life into the world, at least not the one in which I lived. But in Portugal abortion was illegal. Fortunately, I found a midwife who could perform the procedure safely. I was also very lucky that my family didn't find out. As I mentioned earlier, if they had discovered it they would have locked me up and forced me to carry the pregnancy to term.

At the time, Portugal was a deeply Catholic country and church leaders mesmerized the majority of the Portuguese people. I was never swayed by religious morality because it always seemed to be a tool of repression. I was repressing enough on my own to need extra help from a priest or a nun!

Alice Miller's thoughts on religion rang true to me when I read them years later. "When I see the passion with which Catholic priests — men childless by choice — fight against abortion, I can't help asking what it is that motivates them," she writes. "Is it a desire to prove that an unlived life is more important and more valuable than a lived life? [The priests] are acting against life, by misusing the weakness and trust of the faithful and dangerously confusing them. The injunction against abortion goes even further: Consciously or unconsciously, it represents support for cruelty against children and active complicity in the creation of unwanted existences, existences that can easily become a liability for the community at large."[34]

Alice Miller writes about how restricting abortion caused incredible suffering in the Romania ruled by the oppressive dictator, Nicolae Ceaușescu. This incredibly cruel man was penned up in a single room with 10 siblings and was neglected by his parents. And when he rose to power he took his vengeance on the entire nation by forcing women to do what his mother did: "To have more children than they wanted or were able to care for. As a result, Romanian orphanages were full to bursting with youngsters displaying severe behavioral disorders and disabilities caused by extreme neglect. Who needed all those children? No one. Only the dictator himself, whose unconscious memories spurred him

---

[34] *Breaking Down the Wall of Silence*, p. 115

to commit atrocities and whose mental barriers prevented him from recognizing them as atrocities."[35]

I don't have any doubt that my decision not to have a baby was the best choice for me. Alice Miller says that "to force the role of a mother on a woman who does not wish to be a mother is an offense not just against her, but against the whole human community, because the child she brings into the world is likely to take criminal revenge for its birth, as do the many (mis)leaders threatening our lives. All wars we ever had were the deeds of once unwanted, heinously mistreated children. It is the right to *lived* life that we must protect wherever and whenever it is threatened. And it should never be sacrificed to an abstract idea."[36]

I know if I had a child without freeing myself first from the vicious cycle I was in, I would have buried myself even deeper inside the lies and illusions that kept me from reaching my full potential. And, even worse, I would have taken an innocent child with me. My repression would have been complete and I would have passed it down to the next generation. I never would have had the opportunity to leave Portugal, and I always knew in my heart that in order to become free I would have to leave home.

After my abortion I started spending time with a different crowd. Things got even crazier. I hung out with two brothers who lived alone in the house of their dead parents. It was party central, the kind of place people went to score drugs and get laid. I used to steal food from my sisters and cook for these brothers and their drug-addicted friends.

---

[35] *The Truth Will Set You Free*, p. 126–127
[36] *Breaking Down the Wall of Silence*, p. 114

One of the brothers had a job, while the other one was an artist who stayed home all day. I slept with both of them, even though I should have said no to the artist. He snuck into his brother's room one morning after his brother went to work and made his move on me. I should have stopped him, but he was absolutely gorgeous and I was in a bad place in my life. Sleeping with the artist just complicated things, and I knew it was a mistake as soon as it happened. Before and since that experience I've always been monogamous, but at this particular point in my life I had lost all hope and was becoming too numb to really care anymore.

I stayed around the brothers for about a year. The novelty of the situation was wearing off and I knew I needed a change. It was hard being around drug addicts all the time. As Alice Miller writes, "Drug addiction begins with an attempt to escape parental control and to refuse to perform, but the repetition compulsion ultimately leads the addict to a constant concern with having to come up with large sums of money to provide the necessary 'stuff,' in other words, to a quite 'bourgeois' form of enslavement."[37]

I didn't know at the time that my friends were just using their addictions to repress their true feelings even further, but their behavior filled me with a certain sadness. As Alice Miller says, "Every kind of addiction is a way of escaping from the memories of one's own painful life history."[38] While the brothers and their friends used drugs to escape, I knew plenty of people who took more accepted routes and used work, politics, religion and relationships the same way my new friends used sex, drugs and alcohol.

Anyone who's addicted to anything is revealing that they have a false self and that they can't cope with repressed

---

[37] *For Your Own Good*, p. 133
[38] *The Drama of the Gifted Child (1994)*, p. 18

emotions triggered by present circumstances. Their addictions are proof that something is out of balance. As the German-Swiss alchemist and physician Paracelsus established some 500 years ago, "Poison is in everything, and no thing is without poison. The dosage makes it either a poison or a remedy."[39]

Alice Miller says that "every addict can overcome the addiction if she or he is really ready to confront their memories. The manipulative resources of the health care system do not help. As long as a person prefers to live in constant misery rather than face his own history, nobody can help him. But as long as someone remains uninformed of the other options available, we cannot know what she *might* be able to do once society stops encouraging her blindness. It is not just the will to free oneself from addiction that can really liberate a person, as is maintained by Alcoholics Anonymous; it is the will and the determination to find and resolve the *causes* of one's addiction, which always lay hidden in childhood."[40]

Intuitively I knew that being dependent on drugs would make me a slave, and that was the last thing I wanted to be. I had enough oppressors. The only times I allowed myself to drink or do any sort of drug were when I was already feeling happy and strong. I was able to do these things in moderation, without getting addicted, because it was a social activity for me. I wasn't using substances to numb my pain or avoid it in any way. In fact, I've always wanted to understand my pain and figure out where it was really coming from so I could resolve it. I never wanted to rely on drugs to alter my state of mind in order to function in the world.

My time with the brothers, and my eighteen years as a topless dancer, showed me all too clearly how dangerous

---

[39] Retrieved from: http://www.brainyquote.com/quotes/authors/p/paracelsus.html

[40] *The Drama of the Gifted Child* (1994), p. 18–19

drug abuse is. At Bourbon Street I saw and heard the desperation of the other dancers. They became so hooked that they begged for drugs from their dealers or sugar daddies and promised just about anything in return if they didn't have the money to pay for them. Fortunately, I had too much self-respect to go that route.

When I finally stopped hanging out with the brothers and their friends, I was ready to move on to the next chapter in my life. And at about the same time, to add insult to injury, the pharmacy where I was getting birth control pills decided to stop giving them to me without a prescription. I was so pissed off! Like Alice Miller, I saw this as a complete power play. It still bothers me to this day that any sexually active woman needs permission to get birth control. As Alice Miller writes, "Conditioning and manipulation of others are always weapons and instruments in the hands of those in power even if these weapons are disguised with the terms education and therapeutic treatment."[41]

As I mentioned, sex and drugs were just two of the ways I saw the people around me repress their true feelings to avoid the pain of being unloved, neglected children. Religion was another biggie, especially in a country like Portugal. If people could only resolve their childhood repression, the power of religion over us all would crumble like a house of cards.

Sadly, I keep witnessing people who, instead of having to face, see and feel the deep-seated traumas that have been passed down for generations, become obsessed with politics, religion or both. My family is a perfect example of this. They were very susceptible to cults and the repression they offered. Elza, for example, used to make us all pray the rosary every

---

[41] *For Your Own Good,* p. 278

night before bed. She was very strict about it, but there was a funny side to it, too. I think Elza suffered from a sleep disorder because whenever she sat down she'd fall asleep pretty fast. So she'd start the rosary, pass out, wake up really quickly and start over. This would go on for about an hour until she finally gave up. I don't think we ever actually finished an entire rosary!

When I was 15, Elza and Laura befriended a woman name Carolina. She was another nurse who worked at their clinic. Carolina also ran a spiritual center based on the books of Allan Kardec, the French founder of Spiritism. Kardec advanced the idea that the dead are still with us, controlling our thoughts and behavior. Elza and Laura were completely seduced by these occult theories because they gave my sisters an easy explanation for everything. They could blame past lives and bad spirits for all their problems and absolve themselves of any responsibility for their own actions and decisions.

They blamed my rebellious behavior on bad spirits and performed special cleansing rituals on me, hoping to make the demons go away. At first I thought it was funny. Now I had an excuse to act badly! It wasn't *my* fault: Those meddling spirits were controlling me against my will! I was helpless before their power over me!

Of course I knew it was all a bunch of crap — and eventually the whole charade made me extremely angry. I couldn't handle my sisters' lies, their hypocrisy and their ignorance. I've heard all kinds of nonsense from them, things like "I chose my parents before I was born." Or "My suffering is due to the bad things I did in a past life." Or "If you're tired and yawning, you must be thinking bad thoughts and attracting spirits from a low frequency." In modern times, reasonable people don't blame the devil or spirits or past lives for their problems. The extremes to which people go to avoid facing the pain of their own truth — even though such a confrontation would set them free — will never cease to amaze me. "To many people," Alice Miller says, "it seems easier to take medication, to smoke, drink alcohol, preach, educate or treat others, and prepare wars than expose themselves to their own painful truth."[42]

The kinds of superstitions my sisters bought into, while completely crazy, were another way for them to assert their own sense of control — over themselves and over Isabel and me. When I was 20 years old, just after my abortion, it all started getting to me and I began having nightmares. Carolina's daughter, who was my age, told me once that she saw the spirit of an old woman floating on her bedroom ceiling. The image really spooked me and I started incorporating it into my own dreams. Just before I fell asleep, I was convinced I could feel bad spirits around me. I wanted to move, but the spirits wouldn't let me. I started to believe that the spirits returned as soon as I lost consciousness, leaving me paralyzed while they inhabited me. I was so sad and freaked out that I started wearing black most of the time.

Fortunately, I was saved from this madness by going to London as an au pair. The nightmares went away as soon as I left Portugal because I stopped hearing my sisters' crazy, repressive talk.

---

[42] *Banished Knowledge*, p. 148

Worksheet: Start Taking the Power Away from Repression

To protect ourselves from the fear caused by our childhood traumas we repress our pain. While this may be an effective short-term solution, the long-term results can include lashing out at others, finding scapegoats and losing ourselves in destructive addictions to things like alcohol, drugs, sex, work, religion, politics and relationships. The first step toward breaking the vicious cycle of repression is to become aware of the real damage it's causing in our lives.

1. What techniques might you be using to avoid feeling the pain of the child you once were? List any addictions, medicines, spiritual beliefs and behaviors that might be getting in the way of discovering the true cause of your problems.

2. What do you believe would be the worst thing that could happen to you if you faced the fears you've been repressing?

I always kept one foot out of the party scene and never developed a drug problem like most of the dancers. Some of the girls would spend all their time trying to find what they called a sugar daddy. As long as they had a guy taking care of them, they wouldn't have to work. But inevitably, those sugar daddy relationships would fall apart and the girls would have to go back to dancing and start the painful process all over again. There was a dancer who started out at about the same time I did who had a heartbreaking story. She was a lot younger than I was. I was 26 and she was just 18. About a year after we began working at Bourbon Street she got pregnant. She decided to have the baby, even though the father was a loser and had no intention of helping out. She had another baby a few years later with a different loser guy. All the girls told her to quit getting pregnant because she couldn't work at Bourbon Street in that condition. After the second kid was born, this poor dancer got involved with a real lunatic. He sexually abused her little baby and killed it. The night I heard about it I was so disturbed I couldn't dance at all, so I just went home and cried. After that, the dancer disappeared and I never saw her again. I had donated a few hundred dollars to help her out, but she never came back to Bourbon Street to pick up the money we had all raised for her. About a month went by and Bob, the manager of the club, did the right thing and gave us all our money back.

4. Idealization

Repressing our fears and our anger always results in a backlash. We never know when it's going to come, or how it will manifest itself, but it'll definitely show up to fuck with us.

A lot of us do our best to push back the day of reckoning by idealizing our abusers, justifying the pain they inflicted as somehow being good for us. Those who do this end up believing that they needed discipline to set themselves straight. And they often try to validate this belief by achieving some socially accepted form of success.

Overachievers tend to suffer from this syndrome the most. These people are so damaged that they seek to create an illusion of love by winning gold medals, Oscars and other accolades. Athletes who take performance-enhancing drugs, workaholics who burn the midnight oil or step over colleagues to get to the top, and actresses who sleep with people just to get the part are all examples of how the perversion of idealization can get people into trouble.

I'm always dubious of people like Dr. Julio Machado Vaz, Oprah Winfrey, Deepak Chopra and others who gain public admiration for appearing to help people. From my experience, these people are merely using the external trappings of success to run from facing and feeling their own repression.

When we admire people for who they are, instead of for what they have or accomplish, we will have a better society — or at least a more honest one. Those who define themselves by their victories and professional status are on shaky ground, because these things aren't sustainable. But, as Alice Miller says, this *modus operandi* fits "the life of millions of people, brilliant, unconscious, running for the gold ... and never feeling their sadness or rage about their parents who couldn't love them as they were." She goes on to say that we can only lose our symptoms once we become free of wanting to either understand our parents or wanting to help them.[43]

---

[43] Alice Miller Readers' Mail, February 28, 2010. Retrieved from: http://www.alice-miller.com/readersmail_en.php?lang=en&nid=   2991& grp=0210

Just as the overachiever idolizes his or her parents and childhood, so do many other people on the other side of the success spectrum. Many drug addicts feel guilty for being so weak, and for disappointing and disgracing their parents. These people can never blame their parents. Instead, they find scapegoats in themselves, in their children or in society at large.

Another trick we use to avoid our pain and let our oppressors off the hook is to ignore what they did or run away from it like I kept trying to do. We're not necessarily idealizing our childhoods, but in a way we are by refusing to hold the real culprits accountable for the pain we felt as children.

As Alice Miller writes, "It is quite normal for us to owe a debt of gratitude to our parents and grandparents (or the people standing in for them), even if treatment we experienced at their hands was sheer unadulterated torture."[44] After all, we wouldn't be here if it wasn't for them on some level. Our problem is that society's idea of morality emphasizes the value of parents and parent substitutes, often at the expense of the child. "The Fourth Commandment is diametrically opposed to the laws of psychology," Alice Miller writes. "It is imperative that there be general recognition of the fact that enforced 'love' can do a very great deal of harm. People who were loved in childhood will love their parents in return. There is no need of a commandment to tell them to do so. Obeying a commandment can never be the basis for love."[45] Put in an even more compelling way, Alice Miller comments, "... wherever I look I see signs of the commandment to honor one's parents, and nowhere of a commandment that calls for respect for the child."[46]

---

[44] *The Body Never Lies*, p. 66
[45] Ibid., p. 67
[46] *For Your Own Good*, p. 263

It's easy to see how conflicting emotions can get tangled up, resulting in a confused view of our childhood that deflects blame from the people who deserve it most. We'll do whatever it takes to protect ourselves from the terrible realization that we're the children of parents who cannot love. A brutally beaten child, for example, may prefer becoming a serial killer as an adult, instead of accusing his mother or father of brutality.

Alice Miller wrote a lot about how destructive the impulse to protect our parents — especially our mothers — can really be. She believes that women are permitted to be tyrants in the home, punishing "millions of people who will never accuse them of their crimes because almost every child loves his or her mother and would never, never put her in troubles."[47]

Facing personal pain is a lot more difficult than putting mom or dad on a pedestal and blaming ourselves for being a problem to them, or thanking our parents for the cruelty that we've come to believe was necessary to keep us in line.

Alice Miller was frustrated by the fact that the path from being a misled victim to becoming a misleading perpetrator is totally ignored worldwide. She concluded that it's because "almost ALL of us were beaten, and we had to learn very early that these cruel acts were normal, harmless, and even good for us. Nobody ever told us that they were crimes against humanity. The wrong, immoral, and absurd lesson was wired into our developing brains, and this explains the emotional blindness governing our world."[48]

If we could just see with clarity what the false idealization of our childhoods can do to us, it would be easy to admit that

---

[47] *From Rage to Courage*, p. 41
[48] "The Roots of Violence are NOT Unknown." Retrieved from: http://www.alice-miller.com/flyers_en.php

our parents were cruel. Because when we refuse to admit it, we do nasty things to ourselves and to others. We repeat the cruelty that was done to us and find insidious ways to justify it, whether through religion, power, status or some other success marker. Dictators, cult leaders and mass murderers are all links on the same idealization chain. "In order to understand how Mengele was able to remove the eyes and other organs of healthy people, we only have to know what was done to him in childhood," Alice Miller writes. "I am convinced that something almost inconceivably horrible to outsiders would be uncovered, which he himself no doubt regarded as the best upbringing in the world, one to which, in his opinion, he 'owed a great deal.'"[49]

People who idealize their childhoods, or otherwise ignore their pain, have limitless cravings for scapegoats on whom they can avenge themselves for the fears and anxieties of childhood. This is why some people have a lot of children, because unconsciously they want to make sure they have an endless supply of vulnerable, defenseless new victims.

It's fascinating to me that so many of the pro-spanking people I know are also pro-life. They fight so hard for unborn children, only to let these unwanted babies grow up in toxic, abusive environments. Where is the compassion in that? As Alice Miller says, "It is above all the children already born that have a right to life — a right to coexistence with adults in a world in which, with or without the help of the church, violence against children has been unequivocally outlawed. Until such legislation exists, talk of 'the right to life' remains not only a mockery of humanity but a contribution to its destruction."[50]

---

[49] *For Your Own Good*, p. 268
[50] *Breaking Down the Wall of Silence*, p. 115–116

I feel very strongly about a woman's right to choose whether or not she wants to have a child. I don't believe that abortion affects society at large as much as spanking and all other forms of child abuse do. In fact, I believe that it's the exact opposite. Abortion spares the unborn from abuse, and gives women the chance to finally free themselves from the vicious circle of compulsion repetition.

Children are like sponges. They absorb everything their parents repress. And because children are such perfect mirrors of their parents' repression, they're also powerful triggers that put parents into panic mode to keep repressing. No one can trigger in us what's not already in ourselves, but many parents don't want to see that because it would force them to feel the painful truths of their own childhoods that they try to avoid at all costs. Instead, parents force their children to feel what they themselves can't feel. They use their children as scapegoats or "poisonous containers," and endlessly punish them for their bad behavior. Most parents don't take responsibility for the fact that, on some level, they're the cause of their children's bad behavior, due to their own repression.

This is one of the biggest injustices I've ever witnessed in this world. And when this happens, parents lose the opportunity to nurture their children and heal their own hearts. This is very sad and tragic. Parents don't realize that, in most cases, their desire to have children comes from their compulsion to reenact their own childhood dramas — not as victims again but as the oppressors, the ones in control. After all, that's what they were taught when they were children themselves.

I believe that the idealization of one's own parents and childhood is a major obstacle to the betterment of our whole society. Since so many people believe that their parents are always right, it's much easier for them to follow other people in power positions, who cast themselves as mother or father figures disguised as educators, healers, cult leaders, therapists, gurus and government officials.

We become extremely vulnerable when we refuse to face the truth about the people who raised us. Someone with a false self is an easy target for exploitation, which can threaten not only individuals, but also society as a whole. The only thing that can save us is to make sure that more people are true to themselves. We need more people who can fight the power, starting in their own homes. Alice Miller describes these individuals as "people who had the good fortune of being sure of their parent's love, even if they had to disappoint certain parental expectations. Or people who, although they did not have this good fortune to begin with, learned later — for example, in analysis — to risk the loss of love in order to regain their lost self."[51] According to Alice Miller, these people so appreciate their freedom from trauma and tyranny that "they will not be willing to relinquish it again for any price in the world."[52]

When we idealize our childhoods we become just like our childhood abusers and the vicious cycle continues. And we keep holding on to the false hope of eventually gaining love and acceptance from our parents, or from those who stand in to symbolize our parents.

Idealizing the people who raised us puts us in danger, physically and emotionally. Alice Miller believes that the body knows our traumatic history and remembers the cruelty we had to endure as children without being able to really feel it, process it and move beyond it in a healthy way. "... As long as we are compelled to protect our parents we pay our loyalty with our depressions," she writes. But "...by discovering and

---

[51] *For Your Own Good*, p. 85
[52] Ibid., p. 85

understanding the pain of the former neglected child you start to love and cherish him, perhaps for the first time in your life."[53]

She expands on the idea in *For Your Own Good*: "If the tragedy of a well-meaning person's childhood remains hidden behind idealizations, the unconscious knowledge of the actual state of affairs will have to assert itself by an indirect route. This occurs with the aid of the repetition compulsion. Over and over again, for reasons they don't understand, people create situations and establish relationships in which they torment or are tormented by their partners, or both. Since tormenting one's children is a legitimate part of child-rearing, this provides the most obvious outlet for bottled up aggression."[54] This is how the vicious cycle of repetition compulsion has been going on since the beginning of human history.

I never idealized my parents or my sisters in a major way, but I let them off the hook by thinking that things would get better if I could just get away from them. Leaving home and putting an ocean between myself and my family helped me maintain strong, protective boundaries, but it took me almost 20 years to fully cut my emotional ties. At times, I felt that I needed to move to a whole new planet to prevent my family members from getting inside my head and under my skin!

No matter how far away I got, I was still protecting my family by not facing the repressed emotions of the child I once was. I was just caught up in the illusion of trying to find my true self, when my true self was with me all along. I had

---

[53] *From Rage to Courage*, p. 26–27
[54] *For Your Own Good*, p. 263

to learn the hard way that running away didn't help. I was still adapting to the needs of my family: The intensity level was different, but the mechanisms were the same.

Our false self can quickly become our deceptive reality, and as a result we may start behaving in ways we think will be more pleasing to our controllers. Or we might rebel, but even the toughest rebels carry a certain amount of shame and guilt with them. I know I did, and even today I can't say with certainty where my true self ended and my false self began. The lines were blurred in my case. The rebel in me talked a tough game of being true to who I really was, but it was just the mask of a confused, frustrated girl who was scared out of her mind and wished things had been different.

Quite frankly, I wish I could have had a real discussion with my mother, my father, or with Elza and Laura when I was younger. I wish I could have articulated how I felt, to make them understand what they were doing to me. I didn't have the tools back then, so I ran. And even though I now have the wisdom and the courage to explain what I was really going through back then, my sisters still don't quite get it.

Most people give up the fight and retreat into behavior patterns that are more acceptable to the authority figures in their lives. It's a whole lot easier to cave in. I couldn't go that far, but I was still repressing my feelings and acting out my traumas unconsciously, even though I thought I was ahead of the game.

Quite often, despite my reputation in the family as a bad girl, I fell into the trap of trying to be a people pleaser. Thanks to my screwed up upbringing, I tried really hard never to be a burden to anyone. I bought ridiculously expensive presents for my crazy boyfriend Marty just to win his love, hoping to finally get the kind of attention from a man that my father never could give me. In all of my relationships, I was either just as emotionally unavailable as my father was or I went to extremes of trying to make impossible situations work out.

My older sisters and Dr. Julio Machado Vaz had a powerful hold on me, despite my refusal to idolize them and my obvious negative feelings toward them. That's why I moved to London at age 22, to put some distance between us and reinvent myself.

My sister Isabel had moved to London a year or so earlier, after she finished college in Porto, to practice her English and work as an au pair. When she came back she taught English at a private college and was soon asking me if I knew anyone who wanted to work as an au pair in London. "I know me!" I said.

Isabel was reluctant to recommend me. I got mad at her when I realized she could have helped me get a job in London a lot earlier, when she was over there herself. She bought into the party line that I was bad news, a disgrace on the family. But I wouldn't let her get away with it this time. When I pressed her about the job, she told me I needed to get Elza and Laura's permission first, most likely knowing that they'd never let me go.

True enough, Elza and Laura discounted the idea out of hand. They laughed in my face! There was no way I'd go to London and make Isabel look bad with her boss at the college.

I was discouraged, but I was also determined to figure out how to make my escape. Eventually, Elza and Laura decided that my going to London might be a good way to get me out of their hair for a while, and away from all the people they thought were a bad influence on me. If I had responsibilities and was working for a good family, they reasoned, I might actually grow up.

So, much to everyone's surprise, they let me go. I was so excited! On my way to London I was hopeful that the distance from my family would solve all my problems. But my initial hopes for a new beginning were derailed almost as soon as I got there.

My "new family" treated me worse than my brother Carlos and his wife did when I was helping them care for my niece and nephews. I was a slave in this house and it was absolutely miserable. I never had any privacy because the lady of the house would send her kids to my room whenever I was done with the long list of chores she'd given me each day. My only free time was on Sundays — but only if I managed to sneak out of the house before the parents saw me.

During the few times I was able to escape, I rode the Tube all day long. I got to know London pretty well that way, but on more than one occasion I thought I might be better off throwing myself in front of a train than riding on one. The words of Elza, Laura and my other family members rang in my head, and I started to feel like maybe I was as bad as they always said I was.

Jumping in front of a train was a bit too violent for my taste, so I tried to think of other ways I could kill myself. Taking pills was also out of the question. After my last suicide attempt there was no way I could swallow that many pills again. I knew that I had to think of something, because there was no way I was going back to Portugal alive.

Before I could try to take my life again, however, I met a group of other au pairs who gave me a new sense of energy and purpose. The first thing they did was explain British law to me: As an au pair I was entitled to afternoons and weekends off. I couldn't believe how my London family had taken advantage of me. They wanted me around their kids all the time because they wanted no part of them. Both the mother and the father were completely unavailable emotionally to their children.

One of my new friends, Maria, helped me find a better family. These new people lived right next door to where Maria worked, so we got to spend a lot of time together and became really close. For the first time in my life, at age 22 in the city of London, I enjoyed a taste of freedom I had never before experienced.

My new London family took me to see their doctor, who asked me if I wanted to be on birth control. I was so grateful for this opportunity and took advantage of the liberating offer right away. Maria took me under her wing and showed me all around town. One night, she introduced me to a very popular pub in the neighborhood. While we were there I met a guy named Pradeep. He was handsome and shy, and very polite. I liked him right away and didn't hesitate to say yes when he asked me out to dinner.

We had a real nice time together on our first date, but I remember getting into a fight with him over who would pay for the meal. He got really upset when I told him that I wanted to pay for my own dinner. He told me that women never pay in his culture. I told him that the same was true in Portugal, but that I lived by my own rules. And besides, I said, the Portuguese boys never got so upset when I offered to pick up my own tab. Until I know a guy, I explained, I'm not comfortable letting him pay for anything. I never want to be in a position where a guy thinks I'm obligated to sleep with him.

As much as I protested, however, Pradeep won our little argument that night. And he took good care of me during the year or so we were together. Yes, I did sleep with him, but never out of any sense of obligation. I really liked him and, thanks to my new family's doctor, I didn't have to worry about getting pregnant.

Pradeep and I had an interesting relationship. We were lovers who also became pretty good friends. I enjoyed spending my days off with him at his house, just hanging out.

He told me right away that he would have to go back to Kenya at the end of the year to marry a girl who his parents had picked out for him. I didn't understand a lot about his culture, but I did appreciate his honesty.

I didn't like the fact that he was so firmly in the grip of his parents' control. They could never know about me. Once he got really nervous because someone who knew his parents back in Kenya stopped by his house in London while I was hanging out with him. I was in the kitchen cleaning some dishes and I heard Pradeep tell his friend that I was the cleaning lady. At first I was pretty upset and almost confronted the two of them to set them straight, but I took a deep breath and let it go. As soon as the man left, Pradeep apologized profusely for denying our relationship.

Pradeep and I knew that all we had was the present moment, so we agreed to remain faithful to each other until he had to go back home. We had a lot of fun and we both held up our end of the bargain. I look back on those times with great fondness.

It wasn't hard to say goodbye to Pradeep because I knew we couldn't change anything. Besides, the arrangement worked out for me because I was highly commitment-phobic. If any guy started talking about marriage to me, I'd start thinking of nice ways to break up. I'm sure this was because I was so afraid that any man I'd get close to would ultimately let me down like my father had. Let's just say that Pradeep was perfect for me and I was perfect for him.

While Pradeep and I enjoyed our little monogamous illusion during our time together, all the other au pairs were fixated on a tall, blond guy from northern Spain. This guy loved to play the field. All of my friends had one-night stands with him — even the girls who had steady boyfriends.

Discussing this guy's sexual prowess was a game the au pairs played in a tea room next to Edgware Tube Station. When we all got together, whichever girl had slept with the Spaniard the night before would brag about how great he was in bed. Each day a different girl was talking about the great sex she had with the smoldering Spanish boy!

I was naturally curious, although I never found this man particularly attractive. And I certainly didn't care for his personality. He was a very shallow person, with no substance. He was just a robot with no feelings or thoughts. And besides, I was getting plenty of attention from Pradeep to keep me satisfied, thank you very much!

By the time Pradeep left to go back home to Kenya, Maria had moved to Paris and most of the other au pairs were gone, too. Maria's family hired a new girl who was a gorgeous model type from Sweden. She got involved with the husband of the family I was working for, and the affair caused my family to split up.

I had already taken a job at the Talbot Lawn Hotel as a receptionist. It was a fun place where groups of American students lived while studying in London. The next guy I slept with after Pradeep was named Randy. He was a theater student from a college in Rhode Island. I shouldn't have hooked up with him for a lot of reasons. First of all, he drank too much. And secondly, he couldn't stop talking about us being together forever. Commitment alert!

One day I decided to go back to Edgware by myself to check out a pub where we all used to hang out sometimes. It hadn't really dawned on me that I'd run into the Spanish boy, but there he was holding court with a fresh crop of girls. He greeted me with a smile and told me that he was happy to see me. It wasn't long before he asked me if I was still seeing Pradeep. I told him that Pradeep had left for Kenya, and he didn't waste any time before making his move.

Because I had heard so much about this guy from my friends, I agreed to go home with him that night. What a mistake. Honestly, it was the worst sex of my entire life! He was so rough with me I had to stop him in the middle of it and get the hell out of his house.

I guess all those other girls liked it rough, but not me. I like it smooth and soft. From reading Alice Miller's books I understand that people who like rough sex were often spanked as children. So I guess most of my au pair friends had been spanked by their parents on a regular basis!

While I was having fun and exciting adventures in London, I let the good times and new experiences I was having lull me into a state of complacency as far as my family was concerned. The distance between us was actually improving our dynamic. After I was in London for a while, my family was starting to be nice to me and was proud that I was making it on my own.

I was happy to be free from their pressures. Doing what pleased me made it clear that I never again wanted to live under their control. It seemed as long as we lived apart they were nice to me. My older sister Elza even came to visit me in London while I was working at the hotel, and she was impressed that everyone liked me and that one of the professors took us out to dinner with his group of students.

Being in London was a terrific way for me to remove myself from a real solution to my problems and to avoid the emotions I was becoming so good at repressing. But I was just running away without being able to hide. When my visa was about to expire I had to face the hard reality of my former existence. I knew for sure that I didn't want to return to Portugal.

If you haven't figured it out by now, I have a pretty outgoing personality. It was easy for me to make friends with the students at Talbot Lawn. And one of them, a guy named Richard who was studying architecture, agreed to help me get to the United States.

Richard and I weren't romantically involved, and we weren't even sleeping together, but he felt obligated to help me. He got me fired when he broke into the candy machine at Talbot Lawn. I covered for him with my supervisors, but they didn't believe me and gave me the boot. I told Richard — only half joking — that marrying me was the least he could do. He laughed nervously when I made the suggestion, but he actually did go with me to the American Embassy to learn how he could bring his "fiancée" to America.

My plan didn't go any further than that at the time, and I wasn't really getting my hopes up about coming to America. So without a job anymore, I left London and tried to seek employment in France. I didn't have any luck in Paris, so I reluctantly went back to my family in Portugal.

Being home made me more determined than ever to get my butt to the United States. I went to the American Embassy almost every day to get all the documents I needed. They made me get a full physical exam, and they did a background check to make sure I didn't have a criminal record. Everything seemed like it was moving along — however slowly — but I got stuck when they told me I needed someone from the U.S. who would sign a financial responsibility document on my behalf.

I was pretty much completely screwed, so I started looking for work in Porto. I had one interview at a hotel that wanted someone who spoke English, and I had the job until I disclosed that I wanted to move to America in the future. Even though the manager liked me, he said that he was looking for someone who would commit to being there long-term. I was kind of relieved, because if I had gotten that job I probably never would've left Portugal. I knew in my heart that I'd never be happy living there.

I had to get away so I went back to England, traveling as an au pair again with a young Portuguese couple who was going to finish their master's degrees at the University of Reading, not far from London. When we arrived at Gatwick Airport, however, a customs official didn't want to let me in because I'd just been there on an au pair visa.

To convince him that I wouldn't be staying in England, I had to show him my paperwork for moving to America. This came as a shock to the couple I was traveling with, so I had to explain to them that I didn't think my American plan was going to materialize. I was in a lot of hot water with everyone, it seemed, but at least I was away from my family!

About a month after going back to England I stopped by Talbot Lawn to say hello to old friends. In a strange twist of fate, a postcard for me from the American Consulate had arrived at the hotel the very same day. The postcard explained that my case had been transferred from Porto to London. I went immediately to the embassy, where I learned that anyone in the world could sign my financial responsibility form, not just someone from America.

I was ecstatic! Elza was happy to sign the form for me, and as soon as I had it in my hand, I bought a one-way ticket on the next flight from London to a place called Phoenix, Arizona. This was where Richard, my architect friend and almost-fiancé, lived, and it seemed as good a place as any to start my American journey.

I landed at Sky Harbor International Airport at 9:00 p.m. on my 25th birthday. The year was 1984. I tried phoning Richard but got no answer. I'd left London so quickly that I didn't have time to warn him, and as it turned out he was on vacation in San Francisco. After a few hours of calling from a pay phone in the airport, I finally reached his sister-in-law, a woman named Madonna. I explained who I was and she offered to pick me up and let me spend the night. I woke up late the next day not even sure where I was.

Madonna and her husband John had gotten me a birthday cake while I was sleeping, and after a sweet little celebration they took me to Richard's apartment. I waited patiently for him to come back. And when he did a few days later, he was no longer interested in getting married — not even as a way for me to stay in the country.

Of course, I was disappointed. If he had told me this before, I wouldn't have come. But on the other hand, I probably would never have liberated myself if I had stayed back in Portugal.

I didn't know what to do next. I arrived in America with $300 in my pocket and no ticket back to Europe, so my options were limited. There was no way I was calling my family for help, especially now that I was here. I was going to do whatever I had to do to make it in America.

My next move was to contact my friend Randy from Rhode Island, the guy I slept with after Pradeep left London for Kenya. Randy was happy to hear from me, and naturally he was eager to help me out by marrying me. I was nervous because I remembered how obsessed he was over me before, but I really didn't have any other choice if I wanted to stay away from my family.

I arranged to visit Randy in Rhode Island, and when I got there it was immediately apparent that he wanted a lot more from the relationship than I did. For a while I tried to convince myself that I could make a real marriage with him. He was still taking drama classes and wanted to become a famous actor. In London, I used to go with him to all the

Shakespeare plays. His drama teacher invited me to go along, and even bought me a nice suit so I could go with them to all the fancy theaters. Once, I saw Princess Diana in a theater lobby!

But Randy kept pissing me off when I was staying with him in Rhode Island. One morning when I woke up I found a list of chores that he wanted me to do while he was at school. This reminded me of my older sisters and there was no way in hell I was going to be this man's maid. We argued a lot and I started complaining about his drinking and pot smoking. I found a job as soon as I could because I needed to get out of the house. I worked as a live-in caregiver for an older Italian lady and got a second job in a nursing home from 3:00 p.m. – 11:00 p.m.

I stayed with Randy on the weekends, but he was mad at me for spending so much time away from him. Naturally, I was nervous about getting my green card because we were on such shaky ground. On the day we had to go to the immigration office — for the interview to confirm that we were a real married couple — I tried to memorize everything about him and his apartment. While we were in the waiting room, we got into a huge argument. I don't even remember what we were fighting over, but it was a blowout! When the officers called us in, Randy went with one and I went with another. I thought we were in big trouble, but my officer told me straight off: "No further questions needed. I was watching you two. You argue just like a married couple." He smiled at me knowingly, stamped my papers and gave me a permanent green card.

After that, I stopped working for the Italian lady so I could live with my husband, and I got a job in another nursing home close to Randy's apartment. This didn't help our situation and we continued arguing all the time. Once I was mad at him for hanging out with one of our neighbors who happened to be a single mother. He accused me of being jealous, but not a single part of me wanted to sleep with him by then. The final straw occurred when we moved to a sketchy neighborhood in Providence, the capital city of Rhode Island. One night, I was riding my bike home after work and I got robbed by a bunch of guys. I got so scared that I went back to live with the Italian lady I had worked for when I first moved out to be with Randy.

My husband wanted me to come back home, but I knew I needed to end the relationship. I divorced Randy as soon as it was legal for me to do so, which happened to be our first anniversary. I told him I was moving back to Portugal, but I actually headed west to Phoenix because I just couldn't go back home. I had my green card, so I tried giving the United States another chance.

Back in the desert I reconnected with Richard, but we'd go for long periods of time without talking. For the first five years I worked at Bourbon Street he didn't even know I was dancing. One night he just happened to go to the club for a bachelor party and we ran into each other. It was a little awkward for both of us, but after he saw how popular and in-demand I was, I think he was proud that he knew me.

Before I started my dancing career it was tough to make ends meet. When I arrived in Phoenix I first tried working as an au pair again. I found a family, but they needed help 24/7 and the pay was absolutely miserable. Then I tried doing in-home care for the elderly, but that had its own perils — like the priest in a wheelchair who grabbed at my chest and butt every chance he got. Finally, I settled into a job at a nursing home. It barely brought in enough money to pay for a studio apartment, but I was surviving.

For a while, I ended up sharing my small space with a kitchen worker at the nursing home named Chris, who was also looking to cut his expenses. There wasn't much in the way of romance between us, but he was a fairly good-looking guy. Given our tiny living quarters, we quickly became friends with benefits.

It was during that first summer back in Phoenix when a friend of mine from France came to visit me. She wanted to make some money while she was in town, and saw an ad in the paper that said "Waitress Wanted: No Experience Necessary."

She convinced me to go with her to check the place out, and as soon as we walked into Cheetah One I knew that this was no ordinary restaurant. Girls were walking around topless, wearing just skimpy bikini bottoms. Some of them were dancing on tables and some were on stages. At first my friend freaked out and wanted to leave. But I wanted to find out what the owners had to say about the place. I figured it wouldn't hurt just to check it out.

While we waited for the manager we watched the girls dance and noticed how weird their nipples looked. We found out later that the law didn't allow exposed breasts, so the girls covered up their nipples with tiny Band-Aids. Finally, the manager/housemother came out of the back room to talk to us. She looked my friend over from head to toe and was impressed by the exotic look that her French and Tunisian heritage gave her. The housemother explained to my friend that she could make good tips waitressing, but could make twice as much if she was willing to dance.

We went home thinking we'd never go back, but the next day my friend asked me, "What's the big deal dancing topless for men? In Europe, we go topless on the beach all the time!" We spent the better part of the day talking about it, and my friend decided to become a dancer at Cheetah One. I stayed at my low-paying job at the nursing home — making about $30 a day — while she came home every night with about $200 in cash. After about a week or so, I started seriously considering dancing, too.

The first night I did it I was so shy and so scared. The housemother offered me a drink to help me relax. I accepted it, but I resolved that it would be my last. If I had to drink to do this job, it just wouldn't be worth it. And after that first drink, I never had another to get me through a night at the office again.

The next month my French friend got her own apartment and Chris decided to move back to Ohio. With all the money I was making I could almost pay an entire month's rent from a single night of dancing. I was really happy that I finally had financial independence and a safe place where I could be alone with my thoughts and feelings.

I already told you how I made the transition from Cheetah One to Bourbon Street, and how the move doubled my income. When I made the switch I officially began a professional dancing career that would span an incredible 18 years. I became known as the Queen of Bourbon Street and had really found my calling. I was making $400 or more every night — in cash — and I managed to keep my distance from the drugs, sex and crime that were all around me. Dancing all the time kept me in great shape, too. And, most importantly, I was no longer dependent on my family or anyone else for anything.

Having only a sixth-grade education, I thought I was destined for low-paying jobs the rest of my life. I thought that I'd never have complete financial freedom. I tried many times to go back to school, but I always got frustrated and stopped going. I just couldn't keep up, and I was still unaware of my dyslexia. As unconventional as it was, dancing was my personal path to success, and I was so grateful for the opportunity that I put my heart and soul into it.

It was very unusual to start dancing at age 26. Most girls started at age 18 or in their early twenties and many dancers were actually quitting by the time I was just beginning! For a lot of girls dancing was a temporary gig they used to pay for college or to make a quick getaway from a traumatic home life. I used my age and life experience to maximize my earning potential at Bourbon Street. During the hourly two-for-one drink specials, for example, I did my best to avoid serving drinks. Every minute I had to stand in line at the bar to get drinks was tip money down the drain. Waitresses typically got a $1.00 tip, but dancers would get $3.00. Most guys would give me $5.00 for a song because I was so friendly, and I became one of the most sought after dancers in the club.

Thanks to dancing, I started saving money. I was able to buy nice things. I bought my first house. I was also able to support several charities that helped the most vulnerable in our society — children and animals. Unfortunately, I allowed my family to persuade me to give money to my sister Isabel to invest. Part of me knew it was a bad idea, but for the first time I was getting their approval. Back then, their love — or the illusion of it anyway — was still important to me.

Everything seemed to be going my way at Bourbon Street. I really had my shit together and became the go-to girl for other dancers who wanted personal and professional advice. People really couldn't figure me out, but they admired how I stuck to my principles without judging anyone around me. Because of that, and because I was older than most of the other dancers, I became the loving mother figure that some of them had never had.

I was on top of the world. I loved the attention I got from the guys in the club and from the other dancers. I loved the steady supply of cash that was coming my way: Money can be the perfect anesthesia to keep painful emotions repressed. And I loved the daily workout I got from dancing.

What I didn't realize was that I was a ticking time bomb, and that it would take five years until I finally exploded. As Alice Miller describes it, I was just one of millions of bright but unconscious people, striving for success to avoid facing my true sadness and rage toward family members who couldn't love me as I was. I didn't go to the extreme of believing that my childhood was wonderful or that the cruelties and injustices I suffered were somehow justified by loving intentions, but I did let my family off the hook because of my own emotional blindness. I desperately wanted to believe that I was okay and that I didn't need any help.

Worksheet: Put Your Childhood in Perspective

Idealizing our parents or our childhoods — or ignoring painful truths about them — can prevent us from being true to ourselves or from reaching our potential in ways that are truly authentic.

1. Do you strive for excellence in your life to gain approval from family members? Explain.

2. Do you ever try to justify the discipline or punishment that was given to you as a child? Explain.

3. Do you act superior to others in a quest to be right all the time? Do you criticize your friends, your partner or your children unjustly? Write down some examples.

4. Ask the child inside you how you were treated when you were small, helpless and totally dependent on your parents' love. Were you ever spanked or slapped? How did that really feel? Were you ever teased or mocked? How did that really feel?

As much as I tried to focus on work and mind my own business at Bourbon Street, every now and then some unavoidably terrible story would get my attention because it was all anyone could talk about for days. One day a girl named Randi was fatally shot after having sex with a private client. The guy killed himself, too. I couldn't picture Randi at all when the girls were telling me the story. They even tried to imitate her dance moves to help me figure out who she was. It was spooky, but one night after her death she introduced herself to me in a dream. I saw her dancing on stage and she said to me, "I am Randi." This vision still haunts me to this day.

5. Futility

When you idealize your past, or ignore the painful truth by overachieving, hiding behind religious obedience or lashing out at scapegoats, you're fighting a losing battle. What kind of life are you living? When you get addicted to the toxic cocktail created by pain, fear, shame, guilt and repression — no matter how it manifests in your daily life — you're living a futile existence indeed.

A life without freedom is ultimately a useless life because when you hide from the truth the body eventually rebels. "Even if [the body] can be temporarily pacified with the help of drugs, nicotine or medicine, it usually has the last word, because it is quicker to see through self-deception than the mind, particularly if the mind has been trained to function as an alienated self," Alice Miller writes. "We may ignore or deride the messages of the body, but its rebellion demands to be heeded because its language is the authentic expression of our true selves and of the strength of our vitality."[55]

These days, most of us are on a vain quest to improve ourselves. Self-help books and gurus are wildly popular. We believe we can be saved by simple things such as affirmations and positive thinking, but to some degree we end up like Lynne Rosen and John Littig, a husband-and-wife team of motivational talk-show hosts and life coaches who were found dead in their Brooklyn apartment after killing themselves with helium in June of 2013. Their own immersion in the positivity culture couldn't save them.

Alice Miller started to understand why this is so, and we're learning more all the time. According to a *Businessweek* article that reported on the suicide of the positive pair I just mentioned, "A 2012 Canadian study, published in the *Journal of Psychological Science,* found a negative correlation between positive self-statements and mood in people with low self-esteem. As lead researcher Joanne Wood of the University of Waterloo explained, those who try to pump themselves up with such phrases as 'I accept myself completely' end up feeling worse, in part, because affirmations conflict with their own view of themselves. ... As Dr. Wood and others have discovered in studying the psychology of self-esteem, what unhappy people need most is a chance to acknowledge their feelings of negativity."[56]

Alice Miller writes, "With all due respect for everything that has been said and written about the power of love, we should never forget that good will and devout wishing alone

---

[55] *The Body Never Lies,* p. 207

[56] Brady, Diane. "Self-Help Suicides and the Danger of Positive Thinking," Bloomberg Businessweek, June 6, 2013. Retrieved June 2013 from: http://www.businessweek.com/articles/2013-06-06/self-help-suicides-and-the-danger-of-positive-thinking

will not be enough to free a person to love if that person is in a state of unremitting internal war. This desperate conflict would not be taking place if that person's true self had not been suppressed in childhood."[57]

Instead, too many of us think that simply praising ourselves or visualizing ourselves in perfect circumstances is all we need to do to change. Even those who realize that real change is more difficult still take the easy way out and focus their energy on getting rid of symptoms, instead of searching out the root cause. "There are plenty of means to combat symptoms of distress: medications, sermons, numerous 'treatments,' 'miracles,' threats, cults, pedagogical indoctrination and even blackmail," Alice Miller says. "They can all work for a while, but only because they reinforce the repression and reinforce the fear of resolving it. ... A lot of money and fame comes from this business of repression because it satisfies the longing of so many grown-up children: to be loved as a good child. ... In the long term, we have to pay a high price for this repression."[58]

The typical methods people use to search for answers — which are really ways to run away from the truth — are futile because our real, repressed story continues to attempt to make itself heard no matter what we do. Alice Miller believed that our true plight, the root cause of all our repeated problems, will keep trying to gain our attention in more extreme ways until we finally take notice.

Alice Miller describes addiction, for example, as a way for someone in despair to get rid of his or her memory. But this method of self-medication is unsustainable. "This 'solution' is no longer needed if the goal is exactly the opposite, if you want to remember, if you want to feel your plight and to

---

[57] *The Truth Will Set You Free*, p. 48
[58] *Breaking Down the Wall of Silence*, p. 126

understand its reasons, if you slowly become aware of why you were so afraid of acknowledging the reasons," she writes. "This can happen once you decide to stop running away, to stop betraying yourself, to allow the truth to enter your consciousness. You decide to do so because you finally understand that everything else is useless and because you no longer want to watch your life go by before having even begun to live. You decide to stop betraying yourself because you understand that only you can give yourself the love and care you never received and that you can't do that as long as you deny the truth."[59]

They say that whatever doesn't kill you makes you stronger, but I think they have it all wrong. Whatever doesn't kill you makes you weaker, more repressed and more vulnerable to illness and disease.

During my first five years at Bourbon Street, I felt like I had really overcome a lot. I was successful by most financial standards. I was living my childhood dream of having my own place to live. I was the only one of my siblings courageous enough to break the physical chains of repression and move to America. I was no longer under Elza and Laura's thumb and could finally make my own decisions about how I lived my life and who I spent my time with. And the people around me looked up to me for a change. I really thought I had liberated myself from all of the things that bothered me so much as a child and as a teenager.

But it was all an illusion that shattered into pieces when Marty asked me to dance for him. Up until that point, I hadn't really dealt with any of the harm that had been done to me by my family in Portugal in any meaningful way. I may

---

[59] *Breaking Down the Wall of Silence*, p. 127

have pushed it aside for a few years, but I'd done nothing to explore the pain and resentment that was still bottled up inside me. On the outside, I was doing fine. But inside, things were slowly tearing me apart. I realize now that I was actually becoming weaker and more vulnerable, physically and emotionally, while I was away from my family.

I remember the night like it was yesterday. I was dancing on stage, enjoying the hoots and howls of the boisterous but happy crowd, when another girl ran up to me with an urgent expression on her face. She was out of breath and started pointing at a good-looking guy across the room. "Sylvie!" she yelled in my ear. "That young, gorgeous blond guy just paid me to tell you he wants you to dance for him!"

"Tell him that he'll have to wait," I told her. Other guys were ahead of him and it would take me four or five more songs before I could get to him.

Eventually, I worked my way over to Marty. I was incredibly attracted to him, but I was very clear when he asked me out. "I never date my customers," I said. "No exceptions." I did a dance for him, collected my tip and went on my way. I thought that was the end of it, but he had other ideas.

For a guy used to having his way with any girl he wanted, the challenge I presented made me even more desirable to Marty. And as the weeks and months progressed, Marty kept asking me for dances. He often sent other dancers to get my attention, and they all thought I was nuts for being so aloof. At first, it was easy for me to avoid his advances. I was popular at the club and there were always other guys who wanted me to dance for them. When I could make time for Marty I would dance for him. But I always made it clear that he wasn't getting any special treatment.

In Phoenix at that time, customers weren't allowed to touch or have any physical contact with the dancers. But once while I was dancing for Marty, he put his hands on my hips.

I pushed him off and he quickly apologized, but I have to admit that my whole body tingled with excitement. I felt like I had let my guard down, and I wondered at the time if Marty could tell how much I enjoyed his touch.

Marty kept after me, slipping me five-dollar tips with his phone number on them. When other girls offered to dance for him he told them he was waiting for Sylvie, knowing that word would get back to me. I was definitely flattered, but I knew it wouldn't go anywhere because he was too young. He was only 19 and I was already 30. (Full disclosure: I told Marty — and everyone else at Bourbon Street — that I was only 25. And I kept claiming that age — quite believably — for each of the 18 years I worked as a dancer!)

After about four months, all the other girls at Bourbon Street were on Marty's side. They urged me to just go out with the guy. Marty looked, smiled and moved like Leonardo DiCaprio in films like *The Basketball Diaries*, *Romeo + Juliet* and *Titanic*. He had the same hands and body type. The only real physical difference between the two Adonises was that Marty wore his hair a little longer than Leo did.

Marty's good looks and persistence — as well as the constant pressure from the other dancers — ultimately wore me down. But there were other factors in my decision to finally say yes to Marty. For one thing, I realized that hooking up with him could finally give me a reason to end a two-year relationship with my live-in boyfriend, John. John was a nice enough guy, but we were having some problems. I wanted out of the relationship, but I just couldn't figure out a nice way of getting John to move out of my house. I figured if I had a fling with Marty, I could find the strength to finally kick John out of my life.

John was also younger than me, by about five or six years. He was a cop and we met one night in the Bourbon Street parking lot when he was giving someone a speeding ticket. I told him that he looked familiar, and he told me that he'd been to the club a few times with friends on his days off. He confessed that he had a big crush on me from watching me dance, but said he didn't have the guts to ask me out. I told him I'd be happy to meet him for breakfast sometime after work. I had been single for a long time and I liked the fact that this guy had a job.

My last boyfriend was a Mormon named Justin, who couldn't keep a job and was always trying to live off me. He even used my dancing money to tithe to his church! I put up with him for about a year. He was very tall and totally bald from head to toe because of some childhood disease. For some reason, I found him incredibly sexy. His skin was as soft and smooth as a baby's! But he was messed up. A back injury derailed a promising basketball career and his religion was causing major problems in our relationship. Everything was an extreme with him — either he'd get caught up in his church and announce that he couldn't drink a drop or have any more sex until we got married, or he'd just give up and binge like a madman. He couldn't do anything in moderation, and I tried to explain that his erratic behavior was hurting our relationship.

The last straw was when he took me home to meet his family in Provo, Utah, for Christmas. First of all, he made me lie about my career. Second, his parents got mad at me for letting a freezing, stray kitten into their garage. And third, they wanted me to stand up in their church and profess my belief in their religion! It was a nightmare of a trip, but I didn't break up with Justin right away like I should have. He was dependent on me financially, so there was no incentive for him to break up the relationship, no matter how bad it got.

Once, he started choking me when I refused to give him money for a stupid get-rich-quick scheme selling smoke detectors or something. I called 911 and he left the house.

The police came, found him outside and put him in handcuffs. One of the officers came in to see if I was okay and asked if I wanted to press charges. I said no. I ended up taking Justin back in, but the relationship was over. His sister found a job for him in South Carolina and he was ready to move on.

He asked me to co-sign a loan for him because he had no credit and he needed a car for his new gig in South Carolina. I agreed, as long as he promised to leave me alone. Of course, he never made a payment and stuck me with the whole $7,000. I paid off the loan, and it was the best money I ever spent because it got him out of my life once and for all.

So when I met John the policeman, he seemed like a breath of fresh air. He was in great shape. He knew how to use a gun. And he had hair! After John and I met for breakfast, we started dating and went out for the next two years. During the second year he started bringing up the "M" word. As you know, I had issues with making commitments, even though I was quite happy to be in a monogamous relationship and even live together.

Whenever John brought up the topic of marriage, I suggested that breaking up would be a better alternative since I just didn't think we were right for each other. He would always promise to do whatever it took to make it work, but he couldn't even genuinely smile at me! He was so serious all the time, and when I'd ask him to lighten up he just got this weird, fake smile on his face that was downright creepy.

Finally, I stopped sleeping with him. But since we were sharing the living expenses, and because I'm a nice person, I let him have the master bedroom while I took the guest room. I kept telling him he should look for a place of his own, but he was so cheap he wouldn't move out.

Marty was the lever — and the lover — I needed to get John out of the house. Plus, against my better judgment, I thought a little fling with Marty would be an opportunity to have some well-deserved fun. After Justin the crazy Mormon and John Who Never Smiled, I was ready for a good sexual experience, even though I knew better. Once I even told Marty that I couldn't go out with him because he was going to be too much trouble for me. My mind was raising all kinds of red flags, but the pressure of my repressed trauma — and my repressed libido — was too much for my power of reason.

The next time Marty came to Bourbon Street, true to form, he asked me out. But instead of just saying no like I always did, I surprised him with a new response. I told him I was really 31, not 25. I think I was hoping that the revelation would turn him away, but he surprised me by saying it didn't matter. Flustered, I told him I had to get to work.

That night, during my last stage dance, Marty asked me to dance for him at his table. When I went over, I held his face in my hands, kissed him on the lips and finally told him that I'd go out with him. Then I broke the rules again, letting Marty move his hands all over me.

"Can you leave early?" he asked with pent-up sexual energy.

"Of course," I said. "I come and go as I please around here."

Marty took out his wallet to pay for the dance, but I stopped him cold. "From now on my dances for you are free," I told him. "Now that I'm going out with you, you're no longer my customer. I don't date customers outside the club."

That night, sparks flew. Waves crashed against the shore. Marty and I began a sexual relationship unlike anything I had ever experienced. I was older, but Marty was the teacher, putting me in positions I'd never thought possible, until he proved me wrong.

During the first five years of our relationship, I didn't have many expectations of it being anything permanent. He was so much younger than I was and there really were no strings attached. I thought every date could well be our last, but I kept telling myself, "I hope I can see him one more time."

Without even realizing it, I was being drawn deeper into the relationship, longing for the love, approval and emotional availability that eluded me as a little girl. There were glimmers of hope, in addition to our frequent sexual acrobatics, that led me to believe that Marty loved me. But there was a definite dark side to the man I loved, and cracks in the relationship started to form.

For example, Marty would show up whenever he felt like it, unannounced and expecting to fool around. But he became furious at me whenever I tried to do the same. I also caught him going through my voicemail one time, trying to see if I was dating other guys. It wasn't without reason: Marty was often inattentive to me — and sometimes totally absent for months at a time — so sometimes I went out with guys he knew just to make him jealous.

Marty triggered the old behaviors I indulged in after meeting Dr. Julio Machado Vaz, another significant time in my life when I felt no love from the people closest to me. I went out and did what my sisters feared the most, just to test their love and observe their reactions. And when Marty became the most significant person in my life, I did the same thing. Just like my family, Marty wanted me to stay home and be available to him no matter what, as if his life was more important than mine. I tried being good for a while, but after waiting for a long time and feeling unloved, I'd go out and party as an act of rebellion. It was foolish, and without knowing it I became dependent on Marty's love like a child is dependent on the love of his or her parents.

Despite the way he treated me, Marty often complained about how old girlfriends had done him wrong. He played the victim card so I'd feel sorry for him. It was his way of manipulating me into a substitute mother role, always trying to make things better for my little baby. And sure enough, I fell into the same roles of caretaker and victim that my mother played all her life with my father.

I believe that Marty took a perverse pleasure in being condescending toward me. I would often put facts and evidence in front of him, but he'd just refute them and make me feel like I was crazy. He'd claim that I was inventing things, even though I knew what I was saying was true. Just before our final breakup, I had the feeling he had started seeing someone else. And when I showed him the emails that proved it, he still refused to admit it and called me crazy anyway.

Sometimes when I just couldn't take the way he treated me, I'd ask him why he kept asking me out if he was just going to be a jerk. "Because I knew you liked me," he'd say like the complete asshole he was. I'd get quiet because it was true. I did like him. I felt an intense attraction to him from the moment I laid eyes on him. But I wished I could have rewound my life so that I never would have gone out with him in the first place.

At the time, I had convinced myself that the only requirement I wanted in a guy was some basic honesty. I just wanted Marty to respect me enough to tell me the truth. But he wasn't an honest person, and he knew he could get away with being secretive and mysterious. He'd do his little disappearing act and then show up at my house without calling, all nice and fun and cute. Try as I might, I just couldn't stay mad at him. Once he came over in the morning when I was still asleep and tried to get in bed with me. I tried to push him out, and then ran away from him, but he took his clothes off and chased me around the house. The whole episode quickly turned into a sexy farce, and he pursued me until I couldn't stop laughing or resist him anymore.

This roller coaster ride of intense passion and total disinterest on Marty's part left me in a sorry state, just like the one I used to be in when I was a small, defenseless child. I was beyond confused, and all the anger and fears that I'd repressed from my childhood rose to the surface and made me act like a complete fool with this guy. Just a few months after we started dating I went back to visit my family in Portugal. And while I was gone, Marty got back with Lisa, his last girlfriend, and actually moved to Colorado to be with her. I didn't hear from him again until he came back to finish college in the fall of the following year.

At that time, Lisa had left him and he came crawling back to me. I took him in, only to experience some of the craziest years of my entire life. During this time, Marty got arrested for drunk driving and turned to me to bail him out. Rather than see him for the loser he was, I was actually happy that he relied on me so much! So I did what any messed up girl would do: I bought him a $7,000 Honda motorcycle. I know it sounds crazy, but it made me happy to see him happy, even if I was trying to buy his love and affection on an unconscious level.

Interestingly, the motorcycle became a symbol of the power struggle in our relationship. It was something I could take away to punish him, which I did on more than one occasion. It made me feel just like my sister Elza, who used everything she could as leverage to control and manipulate me into being who she wanted me to be. It never worked for me, and I don't know why I thought I could make it work for Marty.

Marty was also attracted to the drug scene that permeated life around Bourbon Street. He loved to party, as long as I kept buying drugs for him. I didn't like it at all, but I felt I had to do it to keep the relationship going. Finally, I stopped buying his drugs and paying his American Express bill every month. I remember saying to him, "If you need some drug to spend time with me, then don't spend time with me at all."

Marty cleaned up his act and actually got a job working in a clean room making microchips. He even started paying for things, and we started spending more time together than ever. He moved in with me and we had some happy times. He worked from 6:00 a.m. to 2:00 p.m., and when he came home we'd have sex before going out to dinner, usually at a sports bar. Sometimes we'd go see a movie and then have sex again before winding down in front of the TV.

Now that Marty was with me all the time I should've been happy. But I was constantly thinking that I needed to get away. Little things bugged me, like his taking charge of the remote control and constantly flipping channels. And bigger things, like his incessant partying with his friends on the nights I worked at Bourbon Street. I started demanding that he be home when I got home from work, and I even threw him out one day when he came strolling in long after the sun had come up. After a few days he apologized, and I foolishly went back for more heartache. In the past when I broke up with someone, I never had the desire to go back. But with Marty it was different. After just a few days away, I'd go crazy with longing for him.

Marty was just like my father. He was nice on the surface, but offered none of the genuine communication I craved. My father and Marty were both passive abusers, who hurt me with a lack of interest. They both neglected me and remained emotionally unavailable. I grew up feeling unwanted, not good enough and not deserving. And in my relationship with Marty I experienced the same things I went through as a child, once again without anyone noticing my suffering or understanding it.

Alice Miller writes that "non-physical abuse can be as harmful as beatings. But it is often less visible."[60] I knew I was feeling hurt with Marty, but it took me a long time to recognize what was going on.

I kept trying to connect and communicate with him, and occasionally he'd say he was listening and promise to change. But more often than not, the actions I expected never came. Sometimes he'd send me an apology email or surprise me with a big bouquet of red roses on my birthday, but that only added to the confusion. Encouraged by these acts of kindness, I'd try harder to connect and communicate. But most of the time, I was talking to a wall. Often, in the most inconvenient places, I'd break down and cry uncontrollably. It would usually be in a sports bar when Marty watched TV rather than talk to me. Like I said before, this painfully reminded me of the time I tried to get my father out of the bar as a little girl and he wouldn't stop drinking.

I turned into something of a nag and did everything I could to control Marty and make him comply. I didn't like the person I was becoming because it reminded me of my mother and sisters. What Alice Miller says is so true — that as long our pain remains repressed we will unconsciously and compulsively do to others what was once done to us. Marty triggered me to act like all the mother figures in my childhood. This in turn reminded Marty of his mother, and made him treat me like his mother had once treated him. It was a vicious circle, all right!

In the book *Thou Shalt Not Be Aware*, Alice Miller writes something that fits Marty perfectly: "It is the dependency of someone who was not permitted to say no because his mother could not bear it, and who therefore refuses all his life to commit himself to his partners in the hope of making

---

[60] *From Rage to Courage*, p. 48

up for what was never possible with his mother — namely, to say, 'I am your child but you have no right to my whole being and my whole life.' Since the seducer is able to assume this attitude toward women only as an adult but not in the early relationship with his mother, his conquests cannot undo his original defeat, and since the pain of early childhood is merely concealed, not cured, by these conquests, the old wounds cannot heal. The repetition compulsion is perpetuated."[61]

Marty was a serial womanizer, and I was a serial forgiver because I was so starved for attention from anyone who I let myself fall in love with. Forgiveness without facing and consciously feeling the repressed emotions of the child we once were is just a cover up of the facts. It's a very seductive trap that keeps us endlessly stuck in our emotional prisons, where we either play the role of the victim or the perpetrator.

There were only two men in my life who made me love them — first my father, then Marty. The drama that played out in both of these deep relationships perfectly explains why I was so afraid of commitment. I didn't want to repeat the pain caused by my father's drinking and his inability to be there for me emotionally. So I didn't care — or maybe I pretended not to care — about Justino, Pradeep, the brothers, Randy, Chris, Justin, John and the other men who attached themselves to my life story.

When I fell for Marty, I made myself as vulnerable as I had been when I was a little girl. And we all know how well that turned out! Marty was perfectly willing to take advantage of me by using me to fulfill his sexual pleasure, enable his addictions and receive expensive gifts. He didn't respect my will or my interests, and it was easy for him to

---

[61] *Thou Shalt Not Be Aware*, p. 80–81

railroad me because I so desperately wanted him to love me. It all boiled down to the fact that Marty was never there for me when I needed him. He was only there when he needed me. And the less he seemed to want me, the stronger my attachment to him grew and the more desperate I became.

This was the pattern of futility I was stuck in for 10 long years. Marty triggered my intense childhood feelings of being unwanted, which had been repressed long ago. Foolishly, I put all my faith in Marty. I relied on him to come through for me despite his constant lies and the way he degraded me without a second thought. There were times when I thought I'd never get out of the mess that I had made for myself.

Worksheet: Where Are You Stuck?

People often find themselves in situations and relationships that loop around in an endless path to nowhere. The compulsion to repeat our childhood dramas is strong when we don't face our repression.

1. From dating womanizers like Marty to starting diets that never seem to last, what are the aspects of your life that you'd like to change but just can't seem to get a handle on?

2. Can you trace the places where you're currently stuck to patterns that troubled you in childhood?

I never judged what other girls at Bourbon Street did on the side, no matter how extreme it seemed to me. It really wasn't any concern of mine, so I always minded my own business and kept my nose clean. I used to say that if people are at peace with what they do and it doesn't hurt anyone, then they should be able to do it. Despite this philosophy, everyone tried to hide their extracurricular activities from me because I was known for being a bit of a prude compared to everyone else. All the girls knew that I was a dancer only. In all my years at Bourbon Street, only one dancer was honest with me: She admitted she would sometimes "fuck customers for money." I appreciated her honesty, and when she got in a fight with her boyfriend once, I let her stay at my house for a few days. Maybe because I lived a pretty clean life I didn't get worn out like a lot of the girls. I actually stayed looking the same the whole time I worked at Bourbon Street — until I was 44 years old. If the business hadn't slowed down and the rules about touching hadn't changed, I probably would have danced for at least four more years. But most of the girls who danced more than a few years would look totally used up, because they didn't have limits and they had the illusion of being able to find a guy to take care of them. I believe that most illusions are dangerous and will destroy us eventually. We can have fun with some illusions for a while if we recognize them for what they are, but we get deeply hurt when we mistake an illusion for the real thing. I remember two older dancers who had been at Bourbon Street on and off for many years. One had a bad gambling problem and lost a lot of money on dog races. The other had a bunch of kids and looked really old. That's probably why she was fired.

6. False Hope

My problems with Marty forced me to look for answers. One night he and his roommate were acting very condescending toward me. Marty often put me down in front of his friends and I hated him for it. Rather than start an argument, on that particular night I decided to go for a walk to clear my head. As I wandered in no particular direction, I kept asking myself why I was still in this relationship and if there was any way to save it.

Before I knew it, I ended up in the self-help section of a nearby bookstore. You've probably figured out by now that I wasn't a big reader, and I was as surprised as anybody to find myself in front of a stack of books. I was that desperate! Until that time, I had only read two books from cover to cover in my entire life. The first was a story about a troubled, drug-addicted girl that I read when I was 19. And the other book was a romance novel that my friend Maria lent me when I was living in Paris.

At the bookstore several titles caught my eye and made me very optimistic. It seemed as if there was nothing that couldn't be solved with a little positive thinking! The book I bought that night was *Codependent No More: How to Stop Controlling Others And Start Caring for Yourself* by Melody Beattie. I didn't know what the word codependent meant, but I really liked the subtitle.

As I read Melody Beattie's explanation of how addiction can impact a relationship, I realized that I had been affected by alcoholics and addicts my whole life. I stayed up all night reading, and in the morning when it was time for Marty to get up for work I shared how his addictions were destroying us both. He didn't pay much attention to what I was saying — he was mostly amazed that I had actually read a whole book in one night!

Melody Beattie recommended a group called Al-Anon, which is a 12-step program for friends and family members of alcoholics and drug addicts. I looked up the nearest meeting and decided to check it out. My experience with this group gave me the cloth of love to wear for a while. And because of the beautiful slogans and prayers they used to lure people in, I masqueraded in this illusion for a long time. I still remember the Serenity Prayer:

"God, grant me the serenity to accept the things I cannot change, the courage to change the things I can and the wisdom to know the difference."

I didn't like how religious the organization was, but as I said, I was desperate to find answers. And they hedged their bets with ambiguous slogans like "A God of your own understanding" and "Take what you like and leave the rest."

Plus, the people in the group seemed so friendly and welcoming. It was such a relief to meet and spend time with other people who at least appeared to be on my side. They gave me hope, and I started to feel happy. Marty was happier, too, because I stopped focusing on him so much. He even seemed to be proud of me for taking positive steps to change things for the better.

I tried hard to get something useful out of my Al-Anon experience by attending weekly meetings for nearly five years. Based on the advice I got from my Al-Anon "friends," I stopped making demands on Marty. I really fell for the idea they espoused that "if we change, they will change." I detached from Marty to focus on the things I could control in my own life. And I tried to love Marty perfectly, so he'd love me in return and become the perfect partner I deserved.

The return on my investment in this group left me frustrated. Al-Anon seemed to work for so many people, but it wasn't helping me at all. At the time I felt as though there was something wrong with me, and the people in the group just added fuel to the fire by blaming me for the problems in my relationship. To preserve their own lies and illusions these people weren't the least bit reluctant to throw me under the bus!

Ultimately, I realized that self-help books and 12-step programs offer a false hope at best. I'm convinced that people who put their faith in these types of things — or in psychologists, psychiatrists or any cult leader for that matter — are avoiding the real causes of their problems and are just masking their symptoms instead. The seductiveness of the quick fixes offered by traditional treatments and therapies is very powerful, and even if they don't work they offer at least temporary relief from the fear and pain of our abused younger selves.

In the best of cases, groups like Al-Anon can momentarily help people cope with unhealthy situations and survive another day inside their emotional prisons, but they can't resolve people's problems. Everyone I encountered in Al-Anon was just reenacting his or her childhood drama like everyone else. The unhealthy, cult-like devotion they invested in the group was actually getting in the way of their true happiness, because the group was just filling in for their parents and keeping them blind to the truth.

In an email to a reader, Alice Miller writes that "even smart people become stuck in confusion for years if the 'healers' demand from them the same as the parents did from the child: to stay blind, to forgive, to make amends, not to make troubles. The fear of the parents, stored up in the body, can make a person obedient and sick forever. I hope that you can overcome this fear by seeing through the hypocrisy of your helpers."[62]

"It is a great mistake to imagine that one can resolve traumas in a symbolic fashion," Alice Miller writes in *The Drama of the Gifted Child.* "If that were possible, poets, painters, and other artists would be able to resolve their pain through creativity. This is not the case, however. Creativity helps us channel the pain of trauma into symbolic acts; it doesn't help us resolve it. If symbolic revenge for maltreatment received in childhood were effective, then dictators would eventually stop humiliating and torturing their fellow human beings. As long as they choose to deceive · themselves about who really deserves their hatred, however, and as long as they go on feeding that hatred in symbolic form instead of experiencing and resolving it within the context of their own childhood, their hunger for revenge will remain insatiable."[63]

Abstract techniques like yoga and meditation only serve to repress our anger and fear even more, making us completely dependent on mantras or daily affirmations every time our anger gets triggered. Don't you think it would be better to ask where our anger and fear come from? What are their real roots? And how can we deal with the causes and resolve them for good? Wouldn't it be nice to free up your energy for real living, instead of wasting it on tools that seem helpful but only keep your anger and fear repressed?

Looking back, I can see how easily I was able to turn my Al-Anon group members into substitute parents. They continued my repression with a confusing combination of

---

[62] Alice Miller Readers' Mail, April 24, 2009. Retrieved from http://www.alice-miller.com/readersmail_en.php?lang=en&nid=   2594& grp=0409

[63] *The Drama of the Gifted Child* (1994), p. 22

love illusions and harsh criticisms, all designed to get me to behave the way I was supposed to. For a time they created an artificial happiness for me, which had the undesired side effect of forcing me to tolerate things from Marty that no one should ever have to tolerate. And then the next minute they'd have their knives out for me. When I finally had a breakdown over Marty's infidelity, they had the nerve to say that it was because I "didn't work the twelve steps hard enough!"

Despite this kind of treatment I stayed with the meetings for a long time, deluding myself that Marty would start his own journey of self-exploration and demolish the walls he had built around himself. I so wanted true intimacy with Marty that I kept going back for more abuse from my group.

Meanwhile, I was reading every self-help book I could get my hands on. You name it, I probably read it! And I was eating it all up, hoping that something would finally work for Marty and me.

The only time I could get Marty's full attention was when we were having sex. So naturally, I'd tell him everything about what I was reading while we were making love. Marty was never selfish in the bedroom, and he even told me that it turned him on when I talked to him in bed. While I went on and on about this or that theory of positive thinking or some such nonsense, he would kiss me, caress me and make love to me with every intention of bringing me to a satisfying orgasm. I'm pretty sure Marty wasn't listening to anything I was saying, because after I'd stop talking during an incredible climax, he'd just get all proud of himself for forcing me to be quiet.

But I kept reading, and talking, and reading some more. I read every word in every book because I didn't want to miss a single clue that could lead me to happiness. And that's how I found Alice Miller. Way back in the bibliography of Melody Beattie's *Codependents' Guide to the Twelve Steps*, I found a reference to Alice Miller's third book, *Thou Shalt Not Be Aware: Society's Betrayal of the Child*. I knew I had to get it because of the subtitle alone, because I had grown up feeling betrayed by everyone in my life. And when I started reading the book, I immediately knew that I had found someone who understood me.

Unfortunately, at the time I was still under the influence of other techniques and treatments that promised a quick fix. The people in my 12-step group kept telling me that all I had to do to change Marty was to change myself, and I was seduced by the simplicity of it — even though I had already gone for years with no results!

I've touched on this a lot in this chapter and elsewhere in this book, particularly in the section about Dr. Julio Machado Vaz — the psychologist who used me for sex — but I really want to reinforce the idea that so-called therapists and gurus only substitute one dangerous illusion for another. As Alice Miller writes, "What can happen when a doctor doesn't stop at self-deception in his flight from pain, but deceives his patients, even founding dogmatic institutions in which further 'helpers' are recruited to a faith advertised as scientific 'truth,' can be catastrophic."[64]

The key to effective therapy is learning how to use your present triggers productively. They can help us clarify, understand and consciously feel our intense emotions within the context of our own childhoods without losing our adult consciousness. A good therapist can help us regain our adult consciousness if we lose it and encourage our autonomy, so we can deal with present issues from an adult perspective. But when a therapist regresses us to the state of the desperate

---

[64] *Breaking Down the Wall of Silence*, p. 34

child we once were and keeps us feeling old pain over and over again, that just reinforces our dependency, keeps us vulnerable to all kinds of manipulations and makes our addiction to pain harder to shake. Why do people keep punishing themselves?

As Alice Miller writes, "... the awareness was borne in upon me that in a state of regression it is not possible to judge the competence and integrity of the person one has turned to for such guidance. This opens up all kinds of opportunities for abuse. The intensive phase with which primal therapy begins is an immediate obstacle to the formation of a balanced, critical, independent assessment of the therapist's abilities by the client. The fact that the attendant uncritical and irrational expectations of healing and 'salvation' can lead to the establishment of totalitarian sects is borne out by the crass example of mass abuse at the hands of the exponents of 'feeling therapy' as described in detail by Carol Lynn Mithers in her book *Therapy Gone Mad: The True Story of Hundreds of Patients and a Generation Betrayed* (1994). But this study was possible only after the community she describes had disbanded, something that frequently takes decades. Today we know that such groups exist and that members of sects are done irremediable harm before they become aware of the fact."[65]

In another book, she goes on to say, "The thing that concerns me most about cult groups is the unconscious manipulations that I have described in detail in my work. It is the way in which the repressed and unreflected childhood biographies of parents and therapists influence the lives of children and patients entrusted to their care without anyone involved actually realizing it. At first glance, it may seem as if what goes on in cults and cultlike therapy groups takes place on a different level from the unconscious manipulation of

---

[65] *Breaking Down the Wall of Silence*, p. xi

children by their parents. We assume that in the former instance we are in the presence of an intentional, carefully planned and organized form of manipulation aimed at exploiting the specific predicament of individuals. ... First, they had learned how to reduce people to the emotional state of the helpless child. Once they had achieved that, they also learned how to use unconscious regression to exercise total control over their victims. From then on, what they did seemed to come automatically, in accordance with the child-rearing patterns instilled into them in their own childhood."[66]

Most people who search for answers never actually find them, because people suffering with their own repression are the ones who practice traditional therapies. Since the beginning of human history, priests, teachers, gurus, psychics, doctors, philosophers and psychologists have all duped people into thinking they could provide real assistance, when it was never possible because the healers were also victims of their own childhoods.

Alice Miller saw the promise of psychotherapy to help people understand why they behave like helpless victims as adults and also to help them take responsibility for their actions. But she was disillusioned when she realized that practitioners couldn't treat patients effectively as long as they failed to deal with their own repression.

The people who write self-help books and lead 12-step groups and otherwise claim to heal people are for the most part little children themselves, afraid to speak the naked truth that could actually lead to true liberation. "I don't see the path to growing but rather the repetition and continuation of the child's dependency on illusions," Alice Miller writes of traditional healing methods. "Growing and healing begin when former victims of mistreatment start to confront

---

[66] *Paths of Life: Seven Scenarios*, p. 142–143

themselves with the cruelty of their upbringing, without illusions about the "love" of a higher power and without blaming themselves for projections. They allow themselves to feel their authentic emotions without moral restrictions and in this way become eventually true to themselves. But the 12 steps continue to keep the ACA [Adult Children of Alcoholics] in the former dependency of the child: fear, self-blame and permanent overstrain. A person who has eventually painfully realized that she was never loved, can, based on this truth, learn to love herself and her children. But someone who lives with the illusion that she was indeed loved by the Higher Power, though she has missed to feel this love, will probably blame herself in the old manner for her lack of gratitude and will tend to demand the love from her children. By so doing, she will pass on the blame to her children if they don't behave in the way she wishes them to do; she will pass on the blame, together with the lie that she learned in her so-called recovery."[67]

It is the major flaw in most human therapies that they are themselves grounded in the fear of the parents and the repressed emotions of traumatic experiences. It's why therapy so often doesn't work, and it frustrated Alice Miller and encouraged her to find a new way. "Sometimes for decades on end, clients and analysts remain bogged down in a maze of half-baked concepts,"[68] she writes. Whether or not a therapist has been freed of his or her own repression is what will determine the success or failure of a given therapy.

Only Alice Miller offers a complete and total solution for our problems because she gets to the root of the matter and frees us from the pain, fear and anger that, if left untreated, can lead us into a state of depression.

---

[67] *From Rage to Courage*, p. 85
[68] *Free From Lies*, p. 132

Worksheet: What Therapies Have You Tried Before?

I was excited to start at Al-Anon because I thought the group had a solution to my relationship problems. But I soon realized that my hopes were misguided. In my experience, I've found that all therapies — from 12-step groups to self-help books to religion — are destined to fail because the practitioners are limited by their own repression. When I was in Al-Anon, all of us group members were reenacting our childhood traumas, even though we bought into the illusion that we were helping each other. Think about the therapies and self-help techniques you've tried to help you live a better life and solve your problems.

1. What therapies have you tried in the past to solve your problems? What self-help books have you read? What organizations have you joined?

2. Were you excited about these therapies, books and organizations when you first started them?

3. Did the therapies, books and organizations you relied on really help you? Did you become disillusioned in any way or come to realize that the only hope they offered was a false one? Were the people involved really free of their own repressed emotions?

When I was doing stage dances I used to jump off and start dancing on customers' tables. The guys all loved the spontaneity and the intimacy of it, and I'd collect a lot of extra tips. Eventually, most of the other dancers followed my lead and started jumping off the stages and into the crowd, too. Bob, our manager, didn't like what was happening because there weren't enough girls on the stages, and whenever he asked one of the dancers to stop jumping off she'd ask him, "How come Sylvie gets to do it?" Bob had Frank, the assistant manager, talk with me about the situation. I told Frank that if Bob wanted me to stop jumping off the stage he should come and tell me himself. Frank said, "I'm telling you to stop because the other dancers are doing it and we can't tell them to stop without asking you to stop, too." I told him that he was just Bob's puppet and said again that I wouldn't stop unless Bob asked me to himself. "And so what if the other dancers are doing it?" I added. "If it works for them and they make money, why can't they do it, too?" Bob never talked to me about it directly, and I kept jumping off the stage and entertaining the clients. Eventually, the other girls stopped doing it because they didn't look as cool and weren't getting extra tips like I was.

7. Depression

When you feel like you can't solve your problems on your own, and when a parade of gurus, therapists and self-proclaimed self-help experts let you down, then depression is likely to hit you hard if it hasn't already done so. It's kind of like what happens when you fall off a diet and end up feeling like a complete failure when you eat more than you've ever eaten in your life. And that's exactly what happened to me in a major way when I realized there was nothing in the world I could do to hang onto Marty, no matter how much I tried to follow the advice of my fellow Al-Anoners.

I had been vulnerable to depression all my life because of my repressed childhood emotions, and I've come to understand Alice Miller's simple formula:

Depression = Self-deception

As long as we deceive ourselves by buying into whatever lies and illusions we use as coping mechanisms — from the idealization of our parents to the cloth of love offered by 12-step groups to the quick-fix, rosy promises of positive thinking — there's a good chance that we'll pay for it with depression, or even worse, like the self-help suicide couple I mentioned in Chapter 5.

This is as true in the United States as it is in Portugal, England, China, Brazil, Russia or any other place inhabited by human beings. For me, one of the best things about Alice Miller's teachings is that they transcend all racial, class and cultural boundaries. Trauma impacts the entire human family, and unless it's properly dealt with, it can lead to tragedy no matter who we are.

All children, no matter where they live, have such a strong need for love that they have no choice but to cling to an illusion if the real thing isn't readily available. How could it be possible for a child, who's totally dependent on his parents for survival, to see the painful truth of their incapacity to love him? A child can never say to her parents, "I don't feel loved by you guys so I'm getting a job and moving out of here." Children often have no choice but to deny their truth, repress their painful feelings and develop false selves in the vain hope that they can somehow earn their parents' love. I've learned that we can't get love where there is none in the first place, no matter what we do.

Every adult in the world has the capacity to give up these illusions and free themselves from the chains of depression that result from emotional repression. Unfortunately, most adults do the opposite. They cling to the false hope of illusions, only to let current events trigger depressive episodes whose root causes are the lingering pains of childhood that haven't been dealt with. Everything we become as an adult is connected to our childhood: Our experiences are a chain of events that bring us to the present moment, for better or worse. A criminal is never guilty just by himself. If society at large could ever find the courage to learn from the chain of events that occurred in each criminal's life from day one, we could prevent many future crimes and a lot of unnecessary suffering.

I spent 10 years of my life trying to earn Marty's love because I thought it was possible, and those were the years I was most depressed. When I look back at pictures of the two of us, I can see the sadness in my eyes. It's like my soul knew the truth all along that Marty was incapable of loving me. But, at the time, I wasn't able to live with the truth that I wasn't loved. I deceived myself into thinking that somehow I was to blame — that if only I could do something differently I'd be able to finally earn the love I craved so much.

Nothing will make us more depressed than believing in lies and illusions. I suffered from depression for years because I tried to believe the lies people were telling me, first from my family and then from those who stood in as substitute parents, namely Marty and the members of the 12-step cult I was a part of. I suffered from depression because I kept allowing others to fool me with their lies and very seductive illusions.

Because we so want to be loved by our parents even as we grow older, it's hard to give up the illusions that we've created to make sense of our traumatic situations. But, as Alice Miller explains, such illusions betray what our bodies know is true: "The cruelty the child had to endure without feeling it."[69]

"It is not the trauma itself that is the source of illness but the unconscious, repressed, hopeless despair over not being allowed to give expression to what one has suffered and the fact that one is not allowed to show and is unable to experience feelings of rage, anger, humiliation, despair, helplessness and sadness," Alice Miller writes in *For Your Own Good*. "This causes many people to commit suicide because life no longer seems worth living if they are totally unable to live out all these strong feelings that are part of their true self."[70]

Alice Miller believed that it takes energy to "repress strong emotions, play down the memories stored in the body, and refuse them the attention they clamor for."[71] That's why we feel so tired when we're depressed, in addition to being angry, irritable, helpless and withdrawn.

My susceptibility to depression really kicked into high gear when I learned that Marty was having yet another affair. It was in the year 2000, at the time I was finally getting my full U.S. citizenship. I felt grateful to Marty for taking time off from work to come to the ceremony with me. When I was done with my speech and went back to where he was sitting, he was gone. I went out to the hall and found him at the end of the corridor, drying tears from his eyes. I thought

---

[69] *From Rage to Courage*, p. 26
[70] *For Your Own Good*, p. 259
[71] *The Body Never Lies*, p. 23

he was moved by my speech, but I found out later what was really bothering him was that he felt guilty about seeing another woman.

His strange behavior continued and I finally came out point blank and asked him if he was seeing someone else. He denied it, but I could feel the force of his lie in every cell of my body. I didn't want to believe it because we were living together at the time and I felt closer to him than ever before. Every morning before he went to work, while I was still sleeping, he kissed me on the forehead and told me that he loved me. And he seemed to be paying a little more attention to all the things I was talking about.

My suspicions were aroused by his actions, however, and I kept my eye out for signs. He started working late a lot more often. Once he came home with highlights in his hair and started using a new line of hair care products. (It turned out his new fling was a hairdresser!) And one day he didn't even come home at all. I got mad because I needed him to come home that day so I could take the car to work.

When these things started to add up, I once again accused him of infidelity. He told me I was crazy. His denial really messed with my head and made me confused because I wanted to believe him, but I knew deep in my heart what was really going on.

So I looked even harder for proof. I found a lot of e-mails from a girl named Amy, but he said she was just a friend. I checked his P.O. Box and found the smoking gun — a wedding invitation for Marty and Amy, with the words "now Marty's new girlfriend!" written on it. The pain that was triggered from being tossed aside was overwhelming. It was exactly how the little girl in me suffered when the grownups didn't take me with them and made me stay behind. I was crushed. I felt betrayed by his friends, too, especially the ones who introduced Marty to Amy even though they had known me for years.

When Marty came home that night I ambushed him as he stood in front of the open refrigerator, trying to decide what to snack on. "I have proof you're seeing someone else," I said, waving the wedding invitation in his face. "What do you think you're doing? You're making the worst mistake of your life — and screwing up all my plans!"

I asked him to get all his stuff together and leave the house immediately. He complied, and waited about a week before he started calling me. I guess we were both feeling some withdrawal symptoms, which is when things got really crazy. He would come by to have sex with me and I'd beg him to stop seeing Amy. But he'd just say that he couldn't and I'd scream at him like a little child, "Why! Why! Whhhyy?!"

One night after being out with his friends and Amy he stopped by my apartment to have sex with me. He was pretty drunk, and after sex he got up to leave. I asked him not to, but he said he had to, probably to go meet Amy again. He ended up getting his second DUI that night. After that, he had to go to jail every night after work and was forced to attend AA meetings, too. On his way to jail he'd stop by my house and have sex with me. I'd tell him that we couldn't keep doing this, and that he had to choose between her and me.

One day I called Amy and told her that Marty would never stop seeing me. At first she didn't say anything, but then she repeated words I heard from Marty 10 years before when he was telling me about his old girlfriend Lisa. Amy said that Marty and I argued all the time and he just couldn't take it.

I replied that it wasn't true, that I let him be most of the time and the only time I complained about anything was when he stayed out too late with his friends. I told her that Marty and I might not be together in the future, but that we still had issues to resolve and she shouldn't get in the middle of it. If she let Marty use her to run away from himself, then Marty would continue to run away from his issues his entire life.

I really hoped that Amy would stop seeing Marty because with her in the picture it felt like my relationship was being violently decapitated. It would have been better if we could have come to a more peaceful end, but Marty didn't have the courage and Amy was only out for her own pleasure as well.

After I hung up the phone with Amy, I wrote her a letter to get a few more things off my chest. I explained that Marty was nervous that I was going to leave him unless we figured out that we wanted the same things out of life. He overheard me tell some dancers that I was going to break up with him, and his typical, immature response was to find the next blind, naïve girl so he wouldn't have to be alone for more than ten minutes. I wrote that Marty was the kind of guy who would take the opportunity to see more than one woman to make sure that he's never without pussy and never has to change.

Writing that letter was a good experience for me. I still wanted Marty to be with me, but getting my thoughts on paper helped me start to see that a healthy relationship was impossible. Still, when Marty finally chose Amy over me, I felt as though a knife went through my heart. I was working so hard with Al-Anon and I really thought I could change things. But when I realized I had wasted five years of my life and nothing was any different, I finally hit rock bottom. Marty had regressed me completely back to the desperate child I once was, unwanted by those I cared for the most. I was absolutely miserable.

I had clung to the hope that Marty and I would make it, despite all the obvious signs to the contrary. And when he ran away with Amy it shattered all the illusions I had that he would ever have the courage to stand up for me. I didn't want to face the fact that Marty was just like my father, but I had to do it if I wanted to really be free.

Worksheet: Understanding Depressed Feelings

Alice Miller believes that depression is a symptom of the repressed authentic feelings of the child we once were, the lies and illusions we believe in instead, and our loss of vitality as a result. Simply put, depression is self-deception.

1. Have you experienced periods of depression, or near depression, in your life?

2. How might you have been deceiving yourself during those times?

3. Whose lies and illusions do you still believe in? Those of your parents? People in the present moment who symbolize your parents?

One girl we called Jasmine was a dancer/ madame who lined up clients for other dancers who were willing to turn tricks. Jasmine's boyfriend was a major drug dealer named Billy, and for a while this outlaw couple would often hang out at my house after hours. I found out later that they came over mostly because their own place was always under surveillance. Some nights, after closing the club, we'd look up and see DEA helicopters circling the Bourbon Street parking lot. But I was still naïve to the scale of things. I really had no idea about the level of wheeling and dealing that was going on around me. All I really knew was that Billy was a very charming, funny Matthew McConaughey-type who always had a lot of cash on hand and traveled with armed bodyguards. He was American, but he spoke perfect Spanish, and twice I traveled with him and a couple of other dancers to Rocky Point in Mexico. We took his boat and partied on the open ocean, getting high while a Jimmy Buffett soundtrack played in the background. I always felt like I was in a movie whenever I was around Billy, and if he hadn't been involved with Jasmine I probably would've slept with him. He was a real charmer and sometimes when he was high he'd say to me, "I look at you and see an angel. As long as you're around, nothing bad ever happens." It turned out that another dancer did fool around with Billy, and when Jasmine found out about the affair the whole group broke up. A few years later I heard that the DEA finally caught up with Billy and sent him to jail for 20 years.

8. Discovery

The beauty of Alice Miller's work is that it reveals a way out of the darkness. It's not a quick fix, and it's not necessarily easy, but the result is true and everlasting.

I wish I had taken advantage of Alice Miller's teachings when I first learned about them in 1996, when I first started to realize that the cracks in the foundation of my relationship with Marty were beyond repair. But I wasn't ready. I was still being seduced — not only by Marty — but also by the illusions of solutions that seemed so happy, positive and simple. None of those things worked for me, and when I hit rock bottom I was finally ready to receive Alice Miller's message.

I couldn't get enough of her when I rediscovered her work, so I began reading every book of hers I could get my hands on. It was such a relief to finally have someone really on my side, confirming what I had always suspected — that my troubles as an adult were caused by my suffering as a child.

Thanks to Alice Miller, I came to understand that the widespread repression of early traumas is the great malady of our society. If we look close enough we can see that this repression is responsible for most of our individual troubles, as well as our societal ills. It appears symptomatically in illnesses, obsessions, addictions, violence, greed, deceit and loss of meaning. And it can lead to cruelty, violence and criminal behavior.

So many of us carry on as if all this perverse behavior is normal, while most of us who really want to find a way out go down the wrong path. All too often, we follow false prophets who get us to believe that eradicating individual symptoms is the way to solve our problems. Little do we know that in doing so we always fail to get to the real heart of the matter — the denial and repression of childhood suffering.

When I read about these ideas in Alice Miller's books, I felt as if this amazing woman was talking directly to me! For once, someone was finally able to cut through all the BS pushed on me by people I could never figure out and through techniques that never worked — that could never work. All these people and techniques did was cement and strengthen the walls of my repression, making me feel like I used to feel as a child — that I was stupid and that something was wrong with me. The fact that I couldn't do the techniques correctly or follow the advice of these people only added to my feelings of guilt and shame. By the time I had fully committed to Alice Miller's teachings I was already starting to feel what I learned I had to feel — the pain I had repressed from my childhood.

My discovery of the truth in what Alice Miller was saying meant that, for the first time in my entire life, I could finally start to love and cherish the little girl I once was. All I had to do was find the courage to acknowledge and feel the repressed emotions of fear, anger and despair caused by the cruelty I had to endure in silence as a child, and then mourn the loss of my childhood. For the first time, I saw that I could free myself from panic attacks, depression, unhealthy attachments to Marty and my family, and a host of other problems.

The year I became a devotee of Alice Miller, she had a new book out — *The Truth Will Set You Free: Overcoming Emotional Blindness and Finding Your True Adult Self.* So that's how I began my reconnection to her writing. I took that new book to the park one beautiful spring afternoon and it really helped crystallize my understanding of what I was going through.

I soaked up every word like a sponge. Every page brought me closer to the truth of my own existence and the illusions that I had so desperately believed in:

- "The real tragedy of people never given the chance to express their needs in childhood is that, without knowing it, they are leading a double life," I learned on page 75.

- Page 96 showed me that "parents often react blindly and destructively because they are still caught up in the reality of their childhood without realizing it."

- The words, "I never cease to be amazed by the precision with which people often reproduce their parents' behavior" struck a chord with me on page 141. "A father will beat his son and humiliate with sarcastic remarks but not have memory whatsoever of having been similarly humiliated by his own father."

- On pages 166 and 167, Alice Miller enlightened me with the idea that if, "… instead of punishment for our errors we received a loving explanation of what was wrong or dangerous about what we had done, we are able to respond with spontaneous regret and integrate the realization that to err is human. But if we were always punished by our parents for the slightest offense, then we integrate a very different kind of knowledge: that owning up to our mistakes is dangerous because it loses us the affection of our parents. The legacy from this experience can be permanent feelings of guilt."

- And on page 179, she really floored me with these words: "Hatred can survive only as long as we feel trapped in the situation of the child who has no choice, who is forced to hold out in hopeless circumstances in order to survive. As soon as the adult sees an alternative, a way out of the trap, the hatred disappears of its own accord. It is then entirely unnecessary to preach morality, forgiveness or exercises in positive feeling. The idea that we can arouse positive feeling in ourselves by engaging in relaxation training or meditation is one that I feel to be profoundly illusory. But again and again I come across advice of this kind, coupled with the assurance that one will free oneself of one's symptoms by forgiving one's parents and substituting positive feelings for negative ones."

Wow. After almost five wasted years with Al-Anon, this really blew me away.

I think the most important thing I learned from Alice Miller at that time in my life was that my intense feelings of despair really had little to do with Marty's most recent betrayal. Sure he was an asshole and treated me wrong, but the situation became a crisis because it had awakened the repressed pain I had felt decades before when I was a defenseless child.

I finally understood that there was a confused little girl inside me who was hurting and angry, and that her feelings of hate and frustration were actually justified. I had been deeply traumatized by those who were supposed to care for me, and if I could just allow myself to feel that and accept it, those feelings would finally start to subside.

If I didn't feel it I'd just keep reenacting my childhood drama, going back to Marty or finding other men who would reject me. As long as people keep on repressing their authentic feelings, the compulsion to repeat will manifest itself in one form or another. I didn't want to do that anymore, so I made a commitment to stay with the intense feelings I had avoided for most of my life and consciously feel them.

I put all my focus on Alice Miller and the idea that it was of the utmost importance to speak the naked truth without manipulative morality or "poisonous pedagogy." Alice Miller used this term to "refer to the kind of parenting and education aimed at breaking a child's will and making that child into an obedient subject by means of overt or covert coercion, manipulation and emotional blackmail."[72]

I let go of all the other self-help books I had read, which were written by people who bought into quaint illusions and hadn't taken the time to deal with their own repression. I had no place in my life anymore for people who told me that alcoholism and addiction were diseases that could be treated. I no longer wanted to be fooled by so-called gurus who preached forgiveness or morality. I was done with mother- and father-figures who shamed people into joining their cults.

In the end it was just me and Alice Miller. She gave me the strength to embark on the final leg of an incredible adventure of self-discovery. All I had to do was feel my pain and move through the intense feelings of my childhood. One part of me was scared. Another part of me was excited. I didn't know what it would be like, but I did know that with Alice Miller's books by my side, I didn't have to go through it alone.

---

[72] *The Truth Will Set You Free*, p. ix

Worksheet: Discover Your Truth

Alice Miller offers a proven method of self-improvement that leads to real and everlasting freedom from the pain, fear, anger, guilt and shame you've been repressing.

1. Are you ready to abandon all the bullshit and finally face the feelings of the child you once were?

One summer, I think it was in 1988, a girl came to work at Bourbon Street who was a recruiter for a gentleman's club in Fairbanks, Alaska. She told all of us dancers that the summers in Alaska were just as busy as the winters at Bourbon Street. She said that we could make a lot more money — more than a $1,000 a night — because the dances there cost $20 a dance, not $5 like they did at Bourbon Street. If you've never been to Phoenix in the summer, consider yourself lucky. It gets hot! Everyone who can gets out of town, so business at Bourbon Street would always get slow. I got interested in seeing Alaska, and the girl kept telling us that the bar was a nice, safe place just like Bourbon Street. She even said that the bar would pay for our plane tickets and give us a place to stay for free! It seemed like an offer too good to refuse, so I decided to give it a try. Once we got to Alaska, a car picked us up at the airport and took us to the club. The housemother asked us for our return tickets and put them in a big safe in a corner of the office. We were all getting a little nervous because the place didn't look anything like we expected. It was more like a brothel than Bourbon Street! Maybe we could make more than a $1,000 a night, but it wouldn't be from dancing. A lot of the girls were stuck because they didn't have money to buy a plane ticket home. I was never happier that I had plenty of money and credit cards. I left the club, went to a hotel and bought myself a plane ticket back to Phoenix. I stayed in Fairbanks for a few days just to see the town, but I never got to see the girls who went with me to Alaska that summer again. I didn't want to visit them at the brothel they were working at, and they never came back to Bourbon Street!

9. Freedom

When Marty and I broke up everything in my life was taking a definite downturn. The dancing business was changing and the money wasn't coming in like it used to. Regulations were being relaxed, and most of the girls at Bourbon Street were doing things with the guys that I just wasn't comfortable with. I had to tell the customers that "no touching" was still my rule, even though the club and the other dancers were allowing it. Bourbon Street wasn't fun anymore. It had become a depressing place to work.

When I first started dancing there was always a long line of young guys waiting to get into the club every night. But starting about 1990 business started to slack off. At first, Monday nights got pretty dead. Then Tuesdays slowed down about a year after that. A few years later, Wednesdays were the next casualty. By the time I quit dancing in 2003, I was only working Fridays and Saturdays. Even those weekend nights — which guaranteed big money in my glory days — were hit or miss in the last months of my career.

In many ways, working less at Bourbon Street was exactly what I needed. I had to have the time and the space to go through my personal dance to freedom. But even before I did my emotional work according to Alice Miller's teachings, I took advantage of my job's flexibility when I was feeling down and depressed.

It may surprise you to know that I used to be a very private person, even as a topless dancer. I could show my body because I knew it was just an illusion. And until I met Marty, I knew there would be no frightening emotional entanglements. Even though all the guys knew who I was and would ask me to dance for them, there was a strange anonymity to my career that allowed me to thrive. Even when I ran into guys from the club in more mundane places like the grocery store or the movie theater, they knew I looked familiar but often had a hard time figuring out how they knew me.

So the job was perfect for me, and I'd only go to work when I felt strong enough to put on a happy face and hide all my pain. Sometimes I'd stay in my house for days at a time, thankful that my career allowed me to come and go as I pleased without having to explain myself to anyone.

Sometimes, when I really needed cash, I'd go and dance no matter how I felt. Going out, moving around and getting positive male attention would often lift my spirits, but other times I'd just go through the motions and leave whenever I got the money I needed. But even when I was just phoning it in, I was careful to make sure that my public persona was always bubbly and energetic. The show must go on!

By the time Marty broke up with me, it was harder for me to work on my own terms because the business had slowed down so much. And to add insult to injury, I had to sell my house and move into an apartment again. The timing was terrible and I missed out on the big housing boom of the mid 2000s. If I had timed it right and had Marty's support, I could have made a profit of at least $250,000 from my home. But when I asked Marty for his advice about what to do, all he said was, "Do whatever you want."

When I heard those words I was pretty raw, and I flashed back to a time when I was 15 years old and in seventh grade. It was the end of the year and my parents were visiting my sisters and me in Porto. I was pretty sure I was doing well in school, so I asked my father to come with me to check my grades. When we looked on the wall I saw that I had failed my physics class — a class I really liked! I came really close to passing, but the F was an F and it really devastated me. I told my father that I wanted to quit and asked for his advice, hoping for some words of love, encouragement and moral support. "Do whatever you want," was his emotionally unavailable reply.

The good thing about losing Marty, my career and my house at the same time was that my expenses were a lot less and I had more time to take an honest look at my life and feel my repressed pain. I tried to go back to my old job as a nursing assistant, but I hated it. The healthcare field just depressed me even more at that time, because by then I understood from reading Alice Miller that the great majority of caregivers were only trying to mask their patients' symptoms with little hope of any real healing. Plus, the math just didn't add up. I could still make more money working two lousy nights a week at Bourbon Street than I could working full-time at a nursing facility.

So there I was, with little to distract me from facing my childhood repression. I was ready, but I wasn't ready for what it was like. Following Alice Miller's direction was not an easy process for me, but the results have made it all worthwhile. Even if it were 1,000 times harder to acknowledge and feel the pain of my childhood, I'd still do it all over again.

When I finally started facing the facts of my history, the repressed emotions of my childhood came out at full force, like lava exploding from a volcano. I cried a lot. I screamed. I ripped apart family photos in violent fits of rage. At times I felt completely beaten up. Some days my body shook uncontrollably, and other days I'd just sit in the dark, crying for hours. It wasn't unusual for me to just lay in my bed in the fetal position and cry so loud that it hurt. Occasionally I'd feel intense hatred, convinced that someone had to die.

When I was going through my intense emotions, it felt like the wires were getting crossed in my brain. Sparks were flying around where they shouldn't have been, frying parts of my mind like a burnt-out circuit board or something. It felt like everything had to be disconnected and then reconnected again.

There really were times when I literally felt like I was losing my mind. I'd get scared that I was going to feel that way forever, and a few times I contemplated suicide again. That's when I had to keep re-reading passages from Alice Miller, who got me off the ledge by reminding me that our feelings can't kill us, no matter how intense they are.

I spent nearly two years in relative seclusion processing, exploring and understanding the roots of my pain — and really feeling it all for the first time. The feelings of the child I once was were far more intense than anything I had ever experienced as an adult. I wanted to stop it all on more than one occasion, but I knew that I had to stay with my hurt until I started to heal.

Feeling the powerlessness of the child we once were is no picnic, which is why so many people aren't able to liberate themselves. The love I had for my cats was seriously the only thing that got me out of bed each day and gave me any sort of purpose while I was going through this turbulent time. Even the people with the courage to try and do it often run back to professional therapists who offer the illusion of assistance without really doing anything. This may feel good in the short term, but they're actually doing themselves a great disservice.

If I had gone to a doctor and told him how I was feeling while I was working through my repressed emotions, I'm sure he would've locked me up and medicated me heavily. He would've prevented my brain from healing, from creating the pathways that had been blocked by neglect and trauma when I was a baby and small child, and later as a teenager who was completely misunderstood and continually traumatized by so-called "professionals" and "helpers."

If I had gone to another 12-step group, they would've traumatized me again with their lies, crazy theories and labels that prevent, rather than promote, true healing.

If I had gone back to the so-called professionals, I'd probably still be trapped today, or maybe dead, because I don't think I would've lasted much longer in a state of dependency. Marty once told me that I was bipolar and that I should take medication. He was just like Elza and Laura, who wanted me to use drugs so that I'd accept their lies without protesting.

I read recently that more than 70 percent of Americans take at least one prescription drug, and that more than half of us are dealing with at least two prescriptions. According to a study by researchers from the Mayo Clinic, antidepressants and painkilling opioids are the most common prescriptions among young and middle-aged adults.[73]

The fact that most people take pills, drink alcohol or use other substances and behaviors to avoid feeling their true feelings just makes me want to scream. As Alice Miller writes, most people "resort to these things to achieve an artificial state of well-being that can divert their attention from unpleasant thoughts, rather than prompting them to try to understand them. So how can they appreciate their true meaning or even try to? How can they realize that these feelings are their true friends, attempting to put them on a track that would lead to self-knowledge? Experience is the only thing that can bring this home to them. You have this

---

[73] "Study Shows 70 Percent of Americans Take Prescription Drugs," CBS News, June 20, 2013. Retrieved from: http://www.cbsnews.com/8301-204_162-57590305/study-shows-70-percent-of-americans-take-prescription-drugs/

experience, and now, to your astonishment, you find that the quality of your life has definitely changed for the better. But you will not be able to explain this to someone in the grip of the products manufactured by the pharmaceutical industry. They will not be able to listen to you ... because they are driven by the panic and fear felt by the children they once were at the prospects of more beatings if they should dare to see the truth or speak out about it."[74]

I've learned through experience that traditional healers can't free people from their problems, because the healers themselves are fully invested in the status quo and scared of their own repressed emotions. Most so-called treatments rely on an avoidance of the past, not a confrontation with it. We're constantly told to let go of the past and live in the present moment. This is the exact opposite of what we need to do, and frankly it's just not possible, as long our emotions remain repressed.

It really bothers me when people — especially trained healers — call painful emotions negative. To me, painful emotions can be very positive because they have the power to reveal our truth. The truth is always positive no matter how much it hurts, because without an awareness of our truth we can't truly heal. Once our painful feelings are understood and consciously felt in the right context and are no longer directed at scapegoats, they start to diminish and are replaced with authentic joy and happiness.

To really live in the present moment and experience that wonderful state of being that Eckhart Tolle calls the "Power of Now," we have to do what Alice Miller discovered: We must go back and explore our past because the knowledge of our true childhood history is the most important part of one's life and the real key to liberation and mental health.

---

[74] *Free From Lies*, p. 161

Alice Miller writes that "if an adult has been fortunate enough to get back to the sources of the specific injustice he suffered in his childhood and experience it on a conscious level, then in time he will realize ... that in most cases his parents did not torment or abuse him for their own pleasure or out of sheer strength and vitality but because they could not help it, since they were once victims themselves and thus believed in traditional methods of child-rearing."[75]

For the first time in my life, after working with Alice Miller's teachings for more than five years, I really did start to see things clearly. I understood why my mother was such a mess and why my father was so unavailable to me. I realized why Elza was so desperate for things to be perfect and why Laura was so domineering. I could appreciate why my brothers in Spain were so oppressive. And I also realized that the jealousy burning in my heart when Marty left me for Amy was really directed at my sister Isabel, not at Marty or his new girlfriend. My family always used Isabel as the model of what a "good girl" should be like, in contrast to the "bad girl" that I was. My resentment at this was at the root of my problems with Marty, and when he rejected me the little girl inside of me cried out for justice.

As a child our repression may be lifesaving, but as an adult it encourages us to do harm to ourselves and to others. So how do you go about resolving your repression? How do you liberate yourself from your own fear, anger, guilt and shame so you can experience real forgiveness and move forward in your life as your authentic self? How do you achieve the kind of truth and vitality that so many religious organizations, therapists, 12-step groups and self-help books fail to really deliver?

---

[75] *For Your Own Good*, p. 249

I did it my own way, and at my own pace, in the privacy of my own home with the help of Alice Miller's books and her website. It was an intense experience, but the good news is that it doesn't have to be as excruciating for you. Marty just happened to be my breaking point, and if I had used milder triggers earlier in my life to resolve my repression I'm convinced that the whole process would have been a lot easier.

According to Alice Miller, a person's repression will keep escalating until it's finally heard. "The truth about childhood is stored up in our body, and although we can repress it, we can never alter it," she writes in *Thou Shalt Not Be Aware*. "Our intellect can be deceived, our feelings manipulated, our perceptions confused, and our body tricked with medication. But someday the body will present its bill."[76]

Marty was like an aggressive collection agency that wouldn't stop harassing me, and I had no choice but to pay up! In a way I'm grateful that I got such a powerful kick in the pants, because otherwise I would have just drifted along in my sorry, repressed state like millions of other people do in our world.

My recommendation to you is to start your personal dance to freedom as soon as you possibly can. If you've come this far in this book there's a good chance that you're 100 times more ready to be liberated from lies and illusions than I was, and that you've already started the necessary brain rewiring. You're already off to a great start!

Now, I'm not a doctor and I'm in no way qualified to give you medical advice, but if it's at all possible I recommend staying off any medication, alcohol or drugs while you're going through your healing process. Those types of substances tend to cloud reality, and for freedom to occur you need to be as real and as raw as possible.

---

[76] *Thou Shalt Not Be Aware*, p. 315

The first thing you need to do to free yourself is to gain an honest awareness of what you suffered as a child and the beliefs you adopted in childhood as gospel truth. You've got to know what you're dealing with, and I hope the worksheets throughout this book have helped you along that path. You'll have another opportunity to do this at the end of this chapter.

As you allow the events of your life to unfold, all that's really required of you is that you observe the feelings that arise naturally to the surface. You don't have to force it — they will come up on their own! Just be sure to brace yourself because you'll likely have to look back and face some painful truths and memories — many of which may shock you.

Were you beaten by your dad?

Were your sisters or cousins mean to you?

Were you abused by an uncle?

Were you made to respond to unkindness in false ways?

Did your mom or dad make you feel ugly?

Did your mom create you to use you as a tool of manipulation to control the man in her life and to secure her own survival? Or to alleviate her own feelings of guilt, anger and shame and to fulfill her own needs for love and attention, instead of loving you and fulfilling your childhood needs? Or did she allow others, or external forces like religion, to manipulate her to have children she wasn't ready to love and protect? Feeling the pain of knowing that we weren't created out of love — and were never loved as children — is the most excruciating pain to face and feel. But avoiding the truth of this pain causes blockages, intensifies our guilt feelings, and supports our blindness and neuroses.

We need to know our whole naked truth; how it really was from the very beginning of our lives. Only by finding the courage to see and acknowledge our painful truth — even if it means losing people we love and being ostracized by others — can we achieve true liberation.

The love we can give to ourselves in this moment gives room for awareness to grow and endures the truth no matter how much it hurts. And only from this basis does love have a chance to develop and grow as a force for good in our lives and the lives of those around us. Love can never flourish if it's smothered in the context of lies, fantasies, illusions, religious hypocrisy and morality — no matter how good, seductive and convincing those things might sound.

Wanting to love and being able to love are two different things. My parents wanted to love my siblings and me, but they didn't get the love they needed when they were children. Because they never learned to love themselves first, they couldn't truly love us no matter how much they tried or wanted to. As Alice Miller wrote, "A mother who is forced to realize that the deprivations imposed on her in her youth make it impossible for her to love a child of her own, however hard she my try, can certainly expect to be accused of immorality if she has the courage to put that truth into words. But I believe that it is precisely this explicit acceptance of her true feelings, independent of the claims of morality, that will enable her to give both herself and her children the honest and sincere kind of support they need most, and at the same time will allow her to free herself from the shackles of self-deception."[77]

When you've inventoried your traumas and identified the real culprits, you'll have to do the hardest thing imaginable. You'll have to feel the pain of the cruelty without making excuses for the perpetrators. Your job is to help the child inside you face its fear or anger, knowing that you're

---

[77] *The Body Never Lies*, p. 21

right there to protect the younger you. You'll want to deflect the feelings, but instead you must experience them.

This is extremely difficult. According to Alice Miller, "The love of a child for its parents is all but indestructible. As children we cannot reconcile this love with the truth, and so we deny that this truth exists. But as adults we can learn to preserve both. In fact we have very little choice, if we want to uphold our verbal tributes to love. It is only in alliance with the truth and the refusal of hypocrisy that authentic love can survive and grow."[78]

The child within you will be afraid to look at past events honestly and will fight you like it's a life-and-death situation. For the child it is life or death, but the adult in you is strong enough to confront anything and everything that ever happened to you. You are no longer defenseless! You have Alice Miller to guide you. And you have me.

Alice Miller published 13 books in her lifetime and you can find many of her blog posts and letters for inspiration online. Please see my list of Alice Miller resources at the back of this book. I list every one of her books, along with a brief review, and I also provide a list of websites you can turn to for additional guidance.

Alice Miller's writing can get a little academic sometimes, and that makes it harder to approach for some people. I wrote this book to make her ideas more accessible to more people, and I hope that you'll be able to use my story to help you find the truth about yourself. You can even email me directly at sylvie@sylvieshene.com to share your story, and I'll try to assist you in any way I can. You can also get great information on my website, sylvieshene.com. I really, really want you to be free! Not just for you, but for our whole society and for the benefit of generations to come.

---

[78] *Thou Shall Not Be Aware*, p. 8

Alice Miller wrote, "If I can feel outrage at the injustice I have suffered, can recognize my persecution as such, and can acknowledge and hate my persecutor for what he or she has done, only then will the way to forgiveness be open to me. Only if the history of abuse in earliest childhood can be uncovered will the repressed anger, rage, and hatred cease to be perpetuated."[79]

If you can find other people in your life to act as enlightened witnesses, so much the better. Anyone who can listen to your story with honesty and sympathy will be a powerful ally. If you can't find anyone to fulfill this role — don't feel bad. I freed myself without anyone's help and you can, too.

I'll be honest with you, some of the feelings at times were so intense that I probably shouldn't have been alone with them. But thanks to Alice Miller's books I was able to understand and move through them. Frankly, I didn't have a choice. Before I discovered Alice Miller I was close to the breaking point, and I probably wouldn't have been able to go on much longer without her writings.

You may not have a choice, either. Regrettably, true enlightened witnesses are hard to come by. To this day I haven't met a therapist I can recommend. All I can really suggest is that you get as much as you can out of this book, and out of all the writings of Alice Miller you can get your hands on.

Just remember this: If particular people or circumstances trigger excruciatingly intense feelings inside you, just keep telling yourself that these are the repressed feelings of the child you once were. Feelings don't kill anyone no matter how intense they are. Only actions kill. So if you ride your intense feelings into shore, direct them at the real culprits

---

[79] *For Your Own Good*, p. 248

who hurt you when you were a defenseless child and avoid taking any actions you may regret later, you'll be free and no one will get hurt.

As an autonomous adult you do have some control over the people you let into your inner circle, and you may have to make some relationship adjustments as you do your emotional work. I took a lot of extra time to be with myself in solitude because most of the people in my life just didn't understand what I was going through. When you're trying to resolve your repression, being around unconscious people who are doing everything they can to avoid their own truths puts you at risk of relapsing into playing your old roles.

Before Marty and I broke up in the year 2000, I was planning an extended trip to Portugal to take care of some family business. But the triggering of my repressed emotions put an end to that plan right away. I knew my family couldn't help me explore and understand my feelings, since they couldn't handle their own. They use every technique available to them to repress their own feelings, and I was afraid — knowing that I was in a vulnerable emotional state — that they'd once again make me their scapegoat, projecting their own repression into me like they did when I was younger.

Sometimes you have to let go of some money or time to free yourself from certain people, like I did with that Mormon guy Justin, but that's nothing compared to your freedom and peace. Other times it may not be practical to show people in your life the exit door, but do the best you can given your specific circumstances.

The real key is to be patient with yourself. Keep trying to focus on your intense feelings and eventually you'll begin to understand them. Once you do, they'll start to subside and you'll start to feel liberated from your old wounds, roles and patterns. You'll begin to realize that any intense, excruciating emotions you feel today are the repressed emotions of the child you once were and have very little to do with your present situation. When a current event or person triggers a strong emotion, you'll be able to take a step back from it. You'll be able to tell yourself that the intense feelings of powerlessness, fear or anger are from the child you once were, and that the present event or person is just a substitute that reminds you of a time when you were really vulnerable.

In the future, you'll no longer be blinded by your repressed emotions. You'll be able to clearly recognize red flags and avoid getting too intimate with people who'll re-enact your childhood drama and have you relive old pains over and over again. You'll be able to better deal with present-day triggers. As a child you were powerless, but as an adult you can obtain the power and the freedom to take care of yourself and get yourself out of abusive situations.

While the child you once were was unable to feel intense fear or anger, it's safe for you to feel these emotions as an adult today. Eventually, you'll no longer feel scared and angry. Just don't give up! You must let your honest feelings show you the true story of what you had to go through as a child.

The thing that really kept me going was the fact that I knew I'd be incapable of loving anybody — especially myself — unless I faced and resolved my repression. I was tired of false starts and sustained failures. The promise of real change gave me the courage to soldier on against the odds.

If you can do the same, then you too will have this incredibly liberating experience, and you'll be truly amazed how much the quality of your life will improve.

By 2003, I was feeling stronger. Every day, the excruciating feelings started to diminish and I found that I could enjoy being around other people again.

I was energized, yet relaxed; confident, without being arrogant. In a word, balanced. Not being trapped inside an emotional prison of my own making I was able to deal with day-to-day problems without connecting them subconsciously to my repressed childhood traumas and blowing them out of proportion. For the first time in my life I was able to keep things in perspective, and was finally free from repeating the drama of my childhood every time something went wrong. I even felt strong enough to return to Portugal. I had come a long way from the 22-year-old who had left her family behind for a new life in London.

My visit lasted a year and a half, and I was able to see my family members for who they were — without being triggered by their projections. In fact, I had a quiet calm about me that everyone noticed. My family could tell that I was a different person and they all had a strange kind of respect for me. They still tried to bring me into their dramas, but I politely refused to get involved.

I finally understood that they, too, were victims of their upbringing. When I was young I allowed them all to convince me that they were superior, that they knew what was better. But when I went back to see them after feeling the true emotions of my childhood, I knew that we were all equals — and that nobody knew what was best for me except me.

While I never expected to get my siblings to change their ways, I was heartened by the fact that some of the younger members of my family were interested in what I had to say. Some of them would take a step forward and then retreat when some repressed childhood feeling got triggered by what I had to say, but they were making an effort and that was a step in the right direction. I tried to explain what was happening to them in a gentle, loving way. Sometimes they understood, and other times they'd freak out and stay away from me for a while.

But usually I wasn't alone for very long because lots of people in my extended family were curious about my newfound freedom. One of my nephews and his wife, for example, were having a hard time handling their two-year-old son's temper tantrums. They both tried to dismiss the child's behavior as the "terrible twos," but I could see that this little boy was in a lot of emotional pain. His father buried himself in his work, and his mother had no idea what her son needed.

When I saw this cute little guy for the first time, both of his parents were trying to force him to stop crying and come give his Great Aunt Sylvie a kiss. I told them it was okay to let him cry and express his unhappiness, and that it's never a good idea to force a child to kiss anyone. I certainly wasn't taking it personally! The boy had never seen me before, so I thought he should at least get to know me first before giving me any kisses. My nephew and his wife backed off, and sure enough the little boy stopped crying.

The next day my niece-in-law said that she had never heard anyone talk about children like I had. From then on she pretty much came to see me every day or asked me to be with her and her child. She didn't want to abuse her son anymore. She wanted to help him and become a better mother.

We spent many hours talking about the pain her son was feeling because his father worked so much, and because for two years he was left in the care of a nanny who, they found out later, was taking psychiatric drugs. When I finally had to return to Arizona, I felt so bad leaving my niece-in-law. I continued to help her via phone and Skype, but one day I wasn't available and she went to her doctor and told him she felt suicidal.

Instead of helping her process and understand the roots of her despair, this doctor put her in the hospital. They gave her strong drugs and kept her there — and away from her son — for an entire month. My nephew was working, of course, so the child was shipped off to his maternal grandparents. When I tried to call him, the grandparents kept me away. They blamed me for their daughter's problems. It was easier to make me their scapegoat than to take responsibility for what they did to their daughter.

I still talk to my niece-in-law on occasion and I admire her for reaching out to me despite the wishes of her parents and my nephew. I know that she's up against some pretty tough odds at home, but hopefully she'll be able to help herself and her son.

Another time during my visit to Portugal I was babysitting for another niece's 4-year-old daughter. The little girl was very hyper because of the abuse she had to deal with, and she lived in constant fear of her parents. While we were playing a game where she was the mother and I was her daughter, the little girl spanked me because I didn't do something she wanted me to do.

"Why are you spanking me?" I asked.

"You're a bad girl," she replied. "You're not doing what you were told."

"Do your parents tell you that? Do they spank you?" I asked.

"Yes," she answered.

I tried to explain to her that spanking is not okay, and that the reason she was being spanked was because her parents were spanked when they were little.

This upset my little grandniece, and with tears in her eyes she said, "You don't understand. Sometimes I'm a *very* bad girl."

"You are not a bad girl," I said. "You're just a little child, and it's not your fault."

Later, this same little girl was walking with me along a very busy street on the way to my sister's house. Testing me to see how I'd handle her if she misbehaved, she refused to hold my hand and wanted to walk alone. This was a very dangerous street with extremely narrow sidewalks, and if she fell into the street she could be run over by a car.

My first impulse was to spank her because that's what was done to me when I was a child, but I witnessed my impulse, acknowledged why it was there and resisted it. Looking for a nonviolent way to solve the problem, I sat the little girl down in front of a store and said, "I'm not moving until you hold my hand."

We sat for a while and I explained why it was so important that she hold my hand. When she agreed, we had a very pleasant walk the rest of the way.

In a similar fashion, I was able to help another grandnephew deal with a painful situation. We were all at my nephew's office when the little boy grabbed a calculator off an employee's desk and wanted to take it home with him. I could feel everyone tense up. They all wanted to grab the calculator and give the boy a slap on the hand. But they restrained themselves because I had been telling everyone about the dangers of hitting children.

The employee told my nephew that his son could take the calculator home and bring it back the next day, but that wasn't an honest solution either. The calculator didn't belong to my grandnephew and it wasn't a toy. So I took charge and sat on the floor with the little boy who was holding the calculator in his hands.

"I know this is going to be painful not to be able to take the calculator that you like so much," I said. "But it isn't yours and we're not going to leave here until you give it back. I also feel disappointed when I don't get what I want and it's okay to feel this way." I helped him accept his feelings, and after about 20 or 30 minutes he understood what I said. Tears ran down his face. Again, I told him that I understood his pain and that it's okay to feel sad, and then he gave the calculator back.

I accomplished all that without resorting to screaming or hitting. Of course I could have grabbed the calculator out of his hands and saved some time, but that would've taught the boy a lesson of violence to pass to the next generation. The circle of violence is hard to break because the compulsion to repeat is so great. But I was able to break it and this is one of my proudest achievements. That day in my nephew's office I gave everyone an example of how to solve a problem without inflicting trauma.

These are just some of the examples of how powerful a helping witness can be, especially for young children. I don't know how all my family members in Portugal will turn out, but I do know that some of them are pretty courageous and that I'm always there to assist them in any way I can.

Today, I feel free and happy 99 percent of the time. My public and private personae are one in the same. I'm living with my truth and I'm free to really love!

Most of my life I felt like I was unwanted, and I think the world lacks true compassion and love because a lot of people feel the same way. Children should never be accidents or mistakes. Because of that I've worked hard to "rebirth" myself, and today I'm proud that I've turned my parents' accident into a life worth living. I no longer feel like my life is a mistake because I now have compassion and love for the child I once was — a child who was rejected from the very beginning, emotionally neglected and used for the needs of adults. Growing up I was constantly lied to and surrounded by perfect hypocrisy, but now the child within me is truly loved and protected by the adult I've become.

When I encounter someone who's acting out their own childhood dramas in a way that can trigger my own patterns, I may get a little annoyed and feel a little sting, but the feeling doesn't last very long. Once I move away from that person or tell them what I will and won't tolerate, I feel good again.

As a child, I couldn't walk away from repressed people. But now, as a mature and conscious adult, I have the courage and strength to walk away — without difficulty — from anyone who's unaware and abusive. I feel like a happy child, but I think like a mature, conscious adult!

Most people don't even try to take out their repression on me, and those who do don't get very far. I'm good at seeing through their lies, games and illusions, and at recognizing the triggers that would have set me into a tailspin before.

I might flirt with an illusion now and then, but I know it's an illusion and I don't get sucked in like I used to. And if I ever feel myself sliding back, a very loud inner voice keeps telling me, "Sylvie! I don't care how seductive this person is or those people are, you need to find the courage to stay away!"

As a liberated individual, you'll have to learn to deal with the fact that the majority of people you encounter won't be free. With people who are still very repressed, I build long bridges and strong boundaries to protect myself. Fortunately, repressed people usually sense that I can see right through them. They feel naked around me and that makes them uncomfortable. Even if there's a physical attraction, they feel insecure and tend to keep our interactions short. I might not get a lot of second dates, but this is fine by me because I'm done being what Alice Miller calls a poisonous container, a depository for someone's rage and insecurities.

The people who try to use and manipulate me usually realize their mistake pretty quickly, and either apologize or head for the hills. My liberation has definitely given me added protection against sociopaths!

Resolving childhood repression is the vaccine against the charlatans of the world who exploit those who are still emotionally blinded by the unresolved, repressed emotions of the children they once were.

Once you're free, your whole outlook on life is going to change. This quote, from a patient of Alice Miller's, expresses what happens perfectly: "The world has not changed. There is so much evil and meanness all around me, and I see it even more clearly than before. However, for the first time, I find life really worth living. Perhaps this is because, for the first time, I have the feeling that I am really living my own life. And that is an exciting adventure. On the other hand, I can understand my suicidal ideas better now, especially those I had in my youth — when it seemed pointless to carry on — because in a way I had always been living a life that wasn't mine, that I didn't want, and that I was ready to throw away."[80]

I've removed all the barriers of false morality and am totally free to experience all my feelings, take them seriously and decide whom, if anyone, to share them with. I've faced my past and can deal with my present circumstances in the context of growing awareness instead of childhood fears.

These words by Alice Miller express how I exactly feel: "If I allow myself to feel what pains or gladdens me, what annoys or enrages me, and why this is the case, if I know

---

[80] *The Drama of the Gifted Child* (1994), p. 82

what I need and what I do not want at all costs, I will know myself well enough to love my life and find it interesting, regardless of age or social status. ... I will know that I have lived my own, true life."[81]

It really is a powerful feeling, and you're likely to find yourself possessing a power that will be threatening to a lot of people. Society is on the side of the status quo, so be prepared. As Alice Miller writes in *Free from Lies*, going against the parents "is a source of major alarm for others ... They will sometimes mobilize all the forces at their command to discredit the former victim and thus keep their own repression intact."[82]

But thanks to Alice Miller, I'm content to be who I am regardless of what other people think. This passage, from *Breaking Down the Wall of Silence*, sums it up so well: "To live with one's own truth is to be at home with oneself. That is the opposite of isolation. We only need confirmation when we are alienated from ourselves and in flight from the truth. All the friends and devoted admirers in the world cannot make up for the loss."[83]

When I die I will not be sad because I have truly lived and will die in freedom, no longer scared and no longer a captive of the emotional prison into which I was born.

What fulfills me now is my mission to bring this valuable information to other people, so they too can have a chance to liberate themselves. I also enjoy sharing my life with others who have the courage to open their eyes and who are able to really see and feel.

---

[81] *Free from Lies*, p. 41
[82] Ibid., p. 30.
[83] *Breaking Down the Wall of Silence*, p. 40

want to make it clear that I'm not telling my story to get sympathy from the world. I'm purely doing it to introduce Alice Miller's books to others, and to show how her books helped me break free. I decided to go public with my story so others wouldn't feel alone like I once did, and to hopefully inspire people to gather the courage and strength to achieve their own freedom.

I constantly witness many people going public with their sad, tragic stories in an effort to manipulate people into feeling sorry for them and feeding their adult compulsions and perversions. They don't want the truth. They only wish to avoid their own pain. These people are exploiting the wounded children they once were, just like their parents or parent-substitutes exploited them when they were defenseless little children. They keep themselves and others endlessly stuck in their childhood dramas, where they play either the role of the victim or the perpetrator.

Alice Miller has proven that we can unlock the emotional doors that hold us and start a glorious dance to freedom. Knowing your own truth and living with it is the best gift you can give to yourself and to future generations. The more healed, or free, you become, the less dependent you'll be. And because people will sense that you're not needy, the more people will be attracted to you. It's kind of ironic, but autonomy is very attractive!

I hope you'll take the challenge to free yourself at last. I hope you'll end your own repetition compulsion naturally — without endlessly staying dependent on crutches like yoga, meditation, religion, 12-step programs, or other pain-numbing addictions.

Starting today, right now, you can use any trigger — a smell, a person, a situation, a touch, a place, a word or anything else that pushes your buttons — as an opportunity to be free. You no longer have to give in to the part of yourself that wants to blame the triggers or hide behind quick fixes. You now have all the tools you need to connect to something deep within you that needs to be confronted, no matter how tempting it is to find a scapegoat or run away.

I'm so grateful to Alice Miller for helping me free myself from my repressed childhood emotions that I've dedicated my life to offering emotional support to others. I'm determined to help you get the information you need to free yourself from lies and illusions, so I'll start you on your journey with these words from the woman who became my enlightened witness through her writings: "It is only after it is liberated that the self begins to articulate, to grow, and to develop its creativity. Where there had been only fearful emptiness or equally frightening grandiose fantasies, an unexpected wealth of vitality is now discovered. This is not a homecoming, since this home has never before existed. It is the creation of home."[84]

I believe in you, and I hope you'll share your story with me.

---

[84] *The Drama of the Gifted Child* (1994), p. 43

Worksheet: Free Yourself from Lies and Illusions

Feeling the pain of your childhood is necessary if you value your life and want to free yourself from repression. I hope this book has been leading you to an honest awareness of the traumas you faced when you were young — and that you can continue on your own dance to freedom.

1. Can you find time to be with your true feelings in solitude? Write down a schedule for working with your emotions. It might be an hour a day, or it might be a week where you go off by yourself.

2. What people in your life will you have to create distance from? Will this be practical? If not, how can you come up with a workable compromise?

3. Write down all the traumas you suffered as a child and the beliefs you adopted in childhood as gospel truth to somehow justify your abuse and suffering. Were you beaten by your dad? Did your mom create you without love to satisfy her own need for love and attention, or because she was forced to have you? Did she make you feel ugly? Were you abused by an uncle? Were you made to respond to unkindness in false ways?

4. Take an honest look at the people who were around you as a child. Whether they're alive or dead, you no longer have to make excuses for them. In what ways did they make you feel scared, angry, shameful or guilty?

5. Let your feelings of fear, anger, shame and guilt rise to the surface without forcing them. Resist every

temptation to deflect them. No matter how intense they are, feelings can't kill you. Your role as an adult is to help the child inside you articulate and feel its repressed emotions, knowing that you're right there to protect the younger you.

If you feel you can't endure the pain alone and must look for a therapist to accompany you in your dance to freedom, I urge you to get a copy of Alice Miller's *Free From Lies* and read the chapter on how to find the right therapist, which starts on page 121. Full disclosure: I looked for a therapist when I was ready to feel my repressed emotions, but I wasn't able to find one who could help me. It isn't easy, even with Alice Miller's tips, because most therapists haven't faced their own truths or resolved their own repression. Alice Miller says that "an 'enlightened witness' is not just someone who has studied psychology or been through primal experience with a guru. In my view, 'enlightened witnesses' are people who have found the courage to face up to their own histories, thus achieving autonomy without having to compensate for their repressed impotence by exercising power over others."[85]

6. As you really experience your feelings and emotions, they will eventually start to subside. Write down what it feels like to be free.

---

[85] *Free From Lies*, p. 121

The Works of Alice Miller:
An Annotated Bibliography

I've read every book written by Alice Miller multiple times. You should see my copies of them — pages are dog-eared and many passages are highlighted! Every Alice Miller book has something to offer people on their paths to freedom and I encourage you to read them all. The first Alice Miller book I ever read was *Thou Shalt Not Be Aware,* and the ones that really clicked for me when I started my journey of discovery were *The Truth Will Set You Free, Breaking Down the Walls of Silence* and *Banished Knowledge.*

Below is a list of every book written by Alice Miller, along with some of my thoughts about each one that I hope you'll find useful. The editions listed below are the ones I used to source the quotes that are footnoted in this book.

Prisoners of Childhood (Basic Books, 1981)

This is the first book Alice Miller wrote and it's the last book of hers that I read. The new edition of this book, retitled *The Drama of the Gifted Child: The Search for the True Self,* made her famous in the United States and is actually a lot easier to understand. *Prisoners* is much more academic and was written at a time when Alice Miller still believed that psychoanalysis could help people resolve their repression. By the time *The Drama* was published, Alice Miller had given up on the illusion of psychoanalysis. She found that its theory and practice actually hindered true liberation because it was just another form of what she called poisonous pedagogy. She was so convinced that psychoanalysis was dangerous that she resigned from the psychoanalytical associations she belonged to.

For Your Own Good (Farrar, Straus and Giroux, 2002)

This is the second Alice Miller book I read. I was attracted to this book by the title because the people who hurt me the most when I was growing up would always say, "It's for your own good." This book answers the question of why some people can be so mean in our world. Alice Miller uses the lives of Hitler, a drug addict and a child murderer to demonstrate how abused, neglected and misunderstood children can grow up to be very dangerous adults.

Thou Shalt Not Be Aware (Farrar, Straus and Giroux, 1998)

I almost wish I hadn't started my relationship with Alice Miller with this book, because it was very difficult for me to get through. But I could still tell that someone was finally speaking the truth based on facts, so I kept reading. It was refreshing to know that there was someone out there who had the courage to tell it like it is! This book helped me understand the consequences of the sexual exploitation of children. I came to see clearly how people who've been sexually abused as children will unconsciously and compulsively enter into exploitative sexual relationships. Most women who get into prostitution, for example, were extremely abused as children and are unconsciously and compulsively telling the true story of what happened to them when they were defenseless. In this book, Alice Miller dissects the lives of famous writers like Virginia Woolf and demonstrates how the abuse they suffered as children comes through in their creative endeavors.

Pictures of a Childhood, (Virago Press Limited, 1995)

In this book, Alice Miller shows how she gained access to her own childhood memories through paintings that show fear, despair and loneliness. Her creative outlet showed her a childhood she never believed she even had! This book really helped me see and feel the fear, despair and loneliness that I, too, had suffered throughout my childhood and youth.

The Untouched Key (First Anchor Books Edition, 1991)

With this book, Alice Miller remains focused on facts and continues removing the many veils that people have used since the beginning of human history to hide the truth. She analyzes the work of famous philosophers like Nietzsche and artists like Picasso, and shows how they symbolically tell the true stories of their childhoods without ever realizing it. Alice Miller believes that the symbolism in their work helped these great thinkers survive, but that it didn't liberate them because they never made the fundamental connection between their ideas as adults and their truths as children.

Banished Knowledge (An Anchor Book, Published by Doubleday, 1990)

I wish I had read this book earlier because it really helped me understand the chains of repetition compulsion and how I kept reenacting my childhood drama in present relationships. Through this book I finally learned that the adult within me had to take responsibility and protect me from further abuse by paying attention to the wounded child who was also within me.

The Drama of the Gifted Child, (Basic Books, 1994)

As I mentioned earlier, this book is the revised edition of Alice Miller's first book, *Prisoners of Childhood*. I like this version much better. Alice Miller shows how gifted, sensitive children end up losing themselves by repressing their strong feelings in order to accommodate the adults around them. The consequences of this can include depression on one end of the spectrum and narcissistic feelings of grandeur on the other.

Breaking Down the Wall of Silence (Basic Books, 1997)

This is another one of my favorite Alice Miller books. It really spoke to me directly and I wish I had read it earlier. The language in this book is much clearer than some of her other books. In a simple way it helped me understand my own history and the real reasons for my adult suffering. More than any other, this book paved the way for my true healing and total freedom. Alice Miller analyzes the lives of many infamous dictators and makes the link between the horrors they suffered as children and the ones they inflicted on their subjects.

Paths of Life — Seven Scenarios (First Vintage Books Edition, 1999)

In the first edition of *Paths of Life*, Alice Miller offers seven case studies. But in the paperback edition, based on new information, she removed the story of a woman called Sandra and the book was called *Paths of Life — Six Scenarios*. When I read Sandra's story in the first edition I felt that something just didn't make sense about her father — and it turns out I was right! In any event, the other case studies do a great job of explaining how our first experiences of pain and love affect all the relationships throughout our lives. This book helped me see how childhood suffering and loneliness prevent people from forming close ties with emotionally honest people. It's only when our repressed fears are faced and resolved — and when our defensive mechanisms have been removed — that we become free to enter into healthy relationships.

The Truth Will Set You Free (Basic Books, 2001)

This is another one of my favorite Alice Miller books. It really helped me stay on my healing path and feel my repressed emotions without being distracted by false philosophies — no matter how seductive they sounded. In this book, Alice Miller explores brain development research and shows how humiliations, spankings and beatings, slaps in the face, betrayals, sexual exploitation, ridicule, neglect and other forms of childhood trauma can cause permanent brain damage. She shows how barriers in the mind — caused by childhood traumas that occurred when our brains were still being developed — make us emotionally blind to the damage done to us.

The Body Never Lies (W.W. Norton & Company, Inc., 2005)

Some people have complained to me that Alice Miller's books are repetitive. It's interesting to me that these same people haven't been able to free themselves and remain stuck in their repressed childhoods without realizing it. Maybe if they kept reading all of Alice Miller's books they'd be able to break through their repression and really liberate themselves! In each book, Alice Miller reinforces her main message in a different light, with new insights designed to help people see themselves and others more clearly and feel things on a deeper level. In this book, Alice Miller shows how religious leaders exploit our fears, use shame and guilt to control and manipulate us just like our parents did, and keep us in the dependent state of the child. She also explains how our repressed emotions can cause health problems in our adult lives.

Free From Lies (W.W. Norton & Company, Inc., 2009)

In this book, Alice Miller shows how we can really free ourselves — and save our lives — by finding the true history of our childhood and recognizing the lies and hypocrisy so prevalent in our society. I loved that she included some of the articles published on her website because it's much easier to read them in the book and digest the insights. This book really helped me permanently remove the invisible reins of guilt, fear and shame put upon me by my childhood abusers, so that no one else could grab them to keep me hostage and chained in their emotional traps.

From Rage to Courage (W.W. Norton & Company, Inc., 2009)

Alice Miller shares the answers to many of her readers' letters in this book. Her honest and compassionate answers helped me clearly see how we can use our strong emotions to reveal the personal truth that makes healing and liberation possible.

Other Valuable Alice Miller Sources

Official Alice Miller Website

www.alice-miller.com

Essays Based on the Work of Alice Miller

http://thesacredmoment.blogspot.com/2006/02/essays-based-on-work-of-alice-miller.html

Andrew Vachss Website

www.vachss.com

The Association For Psychohistory Website

www.psychohistory.com

Project NoSpank

www.nospank.net

My Alice Miller Letters

Alice Miller and I corresponded via email from August 22, 2008, through January 28, 2010. I'm grateful for her wise advice and encouragement. Below are some of my letters and her responses.

August 26, 2008

Dear Alice Miller:

Thank you so much for answering my e-mail. It is surreal to me that I am communicating with you. You are a true hero. And thank you for sending me your new flyer. I will translate and distribute it as soon as possible.

Your suggestion makes a lot of sense. I understand your concerns for my well being with respect to getting stuck in my story, but I think I am strong and mature enough to handle it and protect the little girl within me. I am very well aware of the risk involved, but it's one that I must take.

Anyway, I would like to tell you about the dream I had last night. It is very strange because I don't have many dreams anymore or I just don't remember them. You and I were at the Phoenix airport and you were moving back to Europe. (I know you don't travel anymore, but in my dreams you do!) We were waiting for your plane to take off, but it was taking forever. You were traveling with a cat, and this cat did not need to be in a carrier! He was very calm, followed you everywhere and slept next to you while we waited.

I fell asleep too, and when I woke up you had taken off. I was a little sad that I did not see you leave and did not get to say goodbye. I started to look for my car keys to go back home, but I was having trouble finding them. Eventually I found them in my purse, but when I got out of the airport I was in a strange city and did not recognize anything! I did not feel scared, I just kept looking around in awe, and then I woke up. Do you have any idea what this might mean?

Thank you for your attention and I hope all is well with you.

Much love,
Sylvie

Alice Miller's Response

"Thank you for your letter. You don't mention that you read and understood the new flyer I have sent you. Was the content scaring? The dream may be your unconscious reaction to the scaring flyer. The dream may say: I feel well now, I don't need to know more, I can let Alice Miller go and I can find the key to my car (this is wonderful, it is your autonomy!). But you are a curious person, you are not only looking for your peace, you want to KNOW. This may be the new, unknown city you will now have to discover by writing your book. It is a very encouraging dream."

November 6, 2008

Dear Alice Miller,

I am so excited to find out that you are writing a
new book. I can't wait to read it. Do you know
when you will finish it? And will it be available
in English? I also can't wait until June when
your last book, *Free from Lies* will be available in
English.

You are the most important person in my life
because you are the only one who speaks the
truth, the whole truth and nothing but the
truth. I always knew the truth, but I don't think
I could have been left alone with it much longer.
All my life I was thirsty to hear the truth from
someone else, but everyone I listened to was
telling lies.

Until I read your books: It was the first time that
I knew I was finally hearing the truth from
someone else. I am so grateful to you! Without
you on my side I probably would have been
dead by now. Like J.B. in the "Liberation" post, I
used to hear the same phrases and I too had
difficulty walking away from those people. I
wanted to explain to them and help them
understand. From reading your books, I learned
that I cannot make someone see and understand
if they refuse to see their own truth. Now I can
walk away without difficulty. Finally I am free!
Thank you so much for all your books and your
website.

Much love,
Sylvie

Alice Miller's Response

"Thank you for your letter. I am sorry that my answer to your previous letter didn't appear on the website under your text. I wrote: 'Congratulations to your understanding. You are right, you can't make someone to see who DOESN'T WANT to see.'"

January 2, 2009

In this letter, I asked Alice Miller to comment on some other letters that one of her readers had written to me. The more I get involved on the Internet, the more her response to me rings true!

Dear Alice Miller,

I forgot to tell you, if you like, feel free to comment on the letters I shared with you yesterday.

Best wishes,
Sylvie

Alice Miller's Response

"I have learned over the years of my work on the Internet that there are readers who SEEM to understand SOME of what I have written, at least intellectually, but they are still so afraid of their very cruel parents and of their repressed FEELINGS of rage towards them that they are constantly looking for scapegoats.

"They thus live in continual confusion, pretending that they are healed and even offering help and empathy to others. But eventually they use other

*people unconsciously (even the ones who are quite
friendly to them) as poisonous containers like their
parents did to them, and if the offended people begin
to defend themselves they can become very mean.*

*"I can only urge you to trust your feelings and to
NOT offer your empathy and interest to everybody
just because they say they read and understood
everything I have written. In most of the cases it is a
lie. To understand my books means to overcome the
fear of one's parents, to honestly feel the justified
rage TOWARD THEM, and to no longer use others
to get free from the accumulated rage."*

January 6, 2009

Dear Alice Miller,

The story of the 8-year-old boy here in Arizona
has upset me very much:

> http://www.azcentral.com/12news/news
> /articles/2008/11/26/20081126stjohns-
> boy1126-ON-CP.html

I wished you had elaborated more on your
answer to your reader's letter of 12-2-08, about
the story of the 8-year-old boy here in Arizona.

I identify with this little boy, too.

Heartbreaking. I think this little boy is very
courageous because he took revenge on those
who were hurting him. He did not repress it and
maybe it will prevent him from looking
unconsciously and compulsively for innocent
beings or scapegoats to hurt because of what his

parents did to him. Everywhere I go I find that most people are cowards. They protect and idealize their parents, but they take revenge on innocent beings — other little children, their own children and animals — and help to create wars. Grownups always join together against children. Children are always alone without anyone on their side.

What upsets me the most are the professionals, psychologists and psychiatrists. They all talk about theories but they don't explain to the public the true psychological mechanisms. They hide behind theories so they don't have to face their own painful truth that they are grown men and women still afraid of their own parents.

I have no doubt that the father's friend took the father's side about hitting the little boy. If he had taken the little boy's side and had protected him, this never would have happened.

If a grown person was living in a hostage situation and killed his perpetrators, society would probably take his side, saying that he did what he needed to do to free himself. He would not be punished. Most children live in a hostage situation without anyone to help them. This little boy needed an enlightened witness who could understand and take his side. He does not need more punishment. Maybe I am a little far off, but that is how I feel. As you say: "The parents are the problem and not the children. But nobody wants to understand that parents are not free to give their children emotional support as long as they are stuck in their fear of their own parents and don't dare to question their cruel behavior. Out of this fear, they repeat the cruelties they were subjected to in their own childhoods." (From *Rage to Courage*, page 122.)

I wish that everyone on the planet could read the article on your website, "The Essential Role of an Enlightened Witness in Society."

One more thing, where are all the pro-life people? They spend so much money fighting for the unborn children so that more children are born and used as scapegoats by adults. Why not spend their money fighting for the children who are already here and really need protection? All the pro-life people should read your article, "Protecting Life after Birth" in *Breaking Down the Walls of Silence*, page 113.

Alice Miller's Response

"Thank you for your letter. I completely agree with everything you are writing here. You are right: If an adult who lives in hostage could come free by killing the perpetrator he would have probably not been punished at all. And the child now will be punished or get a therapist who will make him feel guilty for his whole life. This is our system of JUSTICE. Could you send your letter to people of power to make them aware of the absurdity of their system? Your letter should be distributed, wherever you can."

January 8, 2009

Dear Alice Miller,

Today I sent the letter below to Oprah Winfrey. I thought I would share it with you. Also, I'd like to inform you that I have been sending my letter of the 8-year-old boy together with your flyer, "The Roots of Violence are NOT Unknown," to a lot of people and places, including the attorney of the boy, the police department, the courts, President-elect Obama, the U.S. Supreme Court and various news channels.

Thank you,
Sylvie

> Dear Oprah,
>
> I used to be a big fan of yours, but after I read Alice Miller's books I realized that your show is a big illusion. You and your viewers are running from and avoiding personal truths and repressed painful emotions of the little girls/boys inside you. I have stopped distracting myself with TV shows that don't give the full story, the whole truth, or give misleading information. Most people on TV are very articulate and say very seductive words that act like drugs to keep us numb, distracting us from facing our painful truths and from feeling our repressed painful emotions.

Have you read the book the *The Body Never Lies: The Lingering Effects of Cruel Parenting*, by Alice Miller? Your body is telling your truth through symptoms. The reason you keep coming back to the weight issue is because you are not taking the time to pay attention and feel the repressed, painful emotions of the little girl inside you.

Please visit the links below:

http://www.alice-miller.com/flyers_en.php

www.alice-miller.com

I wish you much courage,

Sylvie Shene

Alice Miller's Response

"Congratulations!"

January 12, 2009

Dear Alice Miller,

Thank you.

I wrote this letter a month or so ago, but I did not send it. Here it is now.

Once again, thank you for having the courage to speak the truth. In your post, "B's Forum2" on Monday, September 29, 2008, you wrote that instead of understanding you receive personal attacks. It happens to me all the time. People have told me that you talk about the problem but you don't give any solutions. This is so annoying, because people cannot see or hear the obvious solution that you do give us — the need for each of us to face our personal, painful truths and to trust all of our feelings.

I don't know much about IFS therapy, but all the therapies I have come in contact with actually block us from our true feelings. They merely try to change the present behavior. I have learned that change cannot be accomplished without facing the truth about our past and without working through all our feelings and repressed emotions. Any change at all would just be superficial and temporary.

I'm surprised that "B" has been sucked in by this therapy. Your experience has revealed just how great the compulsion is to repeat, to continue to do to others what once was done to us. I have also learned that people use all kinds of methods, even therapies, to run from facing a personal truth or their true feelings. I would just like to send you a hug.

Love,
Sylvie

Alice Miller's Response

"Thank you for your thoughtful letter. I agree with you that there is a difference between the powerless, legitimate rage of a desperate child that reacts to the cruelty of their parents and the rage of the adult who is attacking others out of denial of their history, by

imitating the behavior of their own parents from the position of 'power' (even grandiosity).

"The first rage (of the child) should be felt and expressed in therapy. It can then be RESOLVED. The second one (of the adult), directed toward scapegoats, can NEVER be resolved (see dictators). If therapists see it as an end point of their therapies and don't enable the patients to confront the early parents and the feelings of that time they do much HARM to them.

"Staying trapped in the hatred toward scapegoats can't be the successful end of a therapy. I hope that you can continue your work if you have this difference in mind and can also explain it in your forum."

February 11, 2009

Dear Alice Miller,

Thank you for sharing your answer to "B.R." I got curious and I went to "B.R.'s" website to read her nasty piece of writing. I did not finish reading it because it bored me to read all about her projections onto you. I am so sorry she is making you her scapegoat. Being someone's scapegoat is never a pleasant thing. I am so grateful for your books and website. Having you here by my side for the last 10 years has been a lifesaver, and it pains me to see someone making you their scapegoat. I hope that you have a good team working with you and that the reader's mail can go on forever. I also hope you have peace and health for many, many, many years.

You know when I read her book and articles and the answers to your reader's mail, which I enjoy reading, I could feel that she was still repressed and harboring illusions. What she was writing was not coming from her true feelings, but from her head. I call people like that parrots — they have great smarts, memories, and are very talented at writing and articulating, but they really don't understand what they are saying. They are not capable of feeling their repressed feelings and they unconsciously project those repressed feelings onto scapegoats.

I had a link on my website at the end of the page of my story to your website and to "B.R.'s" article. I was rereading my story and clicked on the link to the article on your website and got a blank page. For a while I was in a dilemma, not knowing what to do, because I did not want to create a link to her website. I started to write to you to ask you if you could write a small article how religion, spirituality and the 12-step meetings cement childhood blindness. I decided not to bother you and created a link to the article on her website even though I don't agree with IFS therapy (I don't agree with most therapies out there). And now that I have proven my feelings are right, I have a responsibility to not have a link from my website to hers.

If you ever have a chance to write an article about how religion, spirituality and the 12-step meetings cement childhood blindness, I would love to create a link to it.

Again, thank you for being here and for your insights.

Sylvie Shene

Alice Miller's Response

"Thank you for your understanding of what happened. I wrote today an answer under the title 'Aggression out of denial' that could help you maybe to see what happens behind some attacks. I wrote already much about religion, the 12 steps and about blinding people by using poisonous pedagogy, but all this is destroyed in my writing and not focused in a specific article. Maybe I will write some day an article on this topic but I can't promise it now. If you want to publish my answer to E of today on your website you can do it."

November 2, 2009

A pro-spanking person, who was trying to ban me from a discussion thread, wrote this letter to Alice Miller. The pro-spanking people did everything they could to trigger me so I'd lose it emotionally, but once you've truly faced and felt your repression you see through people's games. I may get annoyed and irritated by things sometimes, but people can't break me anymore. This letter accused me of violating Alice Miller's copyright, but as you can see from her response that she was definitely on my side. All my life I've stood alone against the liars, hypocrites and cowards in this world and it felt so good to have Alice Miller defend me like that. I felt so happy knowing that I wasn't alone anymore.

Dear Ms. Miller,

On a "no-spank" thread on Amazon, one of your readers has copied and pasted pages upon pages of your work. One of the copies was of a webpage you allow people to copy and re-post in its entirety, but most of the content seems to end with an "all rights reserved" copyright. In some cases, the person is even copy/pasting the works of your fellow authors and attributing your website, which might not exactly rub them the right way.

> http://www.amazon.com/tag/health/for
> um/ref=cm_cd_et_md_pl?_encoding=UT
> F8&cdForum=Fx1EO24KZG65FC
> B&cdMsgNo=6427&cdPage=258&
> cdSort=oldest&cdThread=
> Tx2RVZKR3QEDU6P&cdMsgID=
> Mx28QB17UEUHKGE#Mx28QB17UEU
> HKGE

We've been concerned about her zeal for copy/paste of copyrighted works for some time, but responsibility dictates that since the poster has failed to see the legal and moral issues, we should at the very least alert you of this.

Alice Miller's Response

"Thank you for your letter and the link. I opened it and found a discussion led very respectfully by Sylvie Shene who seems to understand much about the dangers of spanking that produce, beside other things, ignorant parents in the future. **Of course, the Internet allows everybody to show themselves, their emotional insights as well as their emotional blindness** *(like "I was very much beaten but I turned out very well"). But I didn't find an example of anybody using my name for a text that I have NOT written. Did I miss anything? If you did find this kind of abuse, of disrespecting my copyright, please let me know."*

Acknowledgements

Over the years, many people have either asked me to write a book or suggested that I had a book inside me, waiting to come out. For a long time I dismissed the idea, thinking that I could never overcome my learning disabilities and actually do it. But as I realized how much better my life had become thanks to Alice Miller, and that so many people wanted to talk to me about how I freed myself from lies and illusions, I started thinking that maybe a book could help other people face their own childhood traumas and finally live the lives they were born to live.

What began as this little thought became something I was compelled to complete. I've overcome many obstacles to get this book into your hands. Writing and producing it was a team effort that involved many talented people committed to helping me, and I want to express my deepest thanks to all of them.

Naturally, my most profound gratitude goes to my enlightened witness, Alice Miller, for her honest and courageous work. She is a true heroine. Her books and website saved my life, and I know without a doubt that I would never have liberated myself without her. My goal in life is to get as many people as possible to learn the truth that she discovered.

Second, I'd like to thank my co-writer, Ed Sweet, for having the courage and patience to work with me. Without his vital assistance, writing expertise and professionalism, this book would never have been possible. It was the most perfect collaboration.

I also want to thank Jon Roemer in San Francisco for his assistance and writing skills, which helped get me over a small bump in the road during the creative process. Jon was in the right place at the right time for me!

In fact, so many people were in the right place at the right time in my life that it's hard to mention all of them. Of course, I have to thank Richard in Phoenix, who brought me to America. Without his assistance and friendship, I would have stayed in Europe and probably never would have found my way to Alice Miller. Getting to the United States was so important because I was desperate to distance myself from my family. Richard was like a life preserver you throw at someone who's drowning in dangerous waters.

Randy, my husband in Rhode Island, was also helpful to me in a similar way. Our marriage allowed me to stay in America and freed me up to find my path to Alice Miller.

I probably owe my freedom to my ex-boyfriend Marty more than anyone. His triggering of my childhood repression forced me to look for answers. My longing for his love and my desire to learn to love him perfectly forced me to lift up every stone in search of a solution. Even though our relationship couldn't be saved at the end, I was able to ally with the wounded child inside of me and free myself from the emotional prison I was born into. I consider Marty the biological father of this book, which is my baby, as well as my gift to the world.

I never would have met Marty if it hadn't been for Bob at Bourbon Street in Phoenix. He not only hired me as a 26-year-old — an age when most dancers have long since retired — but he was also so confident in my abilities that he let me come and go as I pleased and innovate ways to entertain the clients and make more money for myself. I would never have lasted 18 years at Bourbon Street without the freedom to be myself, and I'm grateful to Bob for staying out of my way.

I really enjoyed working at Bourbon Street, and I'd like to thank all the other dancers for being friendly with me and making it such a fun and exciting experience. I have to apologize for all the times I bumped into my co-workers while trying to get from the tables to the stages on time! I also want to thank all the DJs, especially Kiante and Jeff, for playing great music on my stages. They were the best! And big thanks also go to all the bartenders, housemothers and the doormen who kept an eye on me and made sure I was always safe by walking me to my car every night.

My life has changed since my days at Bourbon Street. It's a lot quieter, but my relationships are a lot deeper. That's why I'm so grateful to my friend Rosetta Fricano, who's been so supportive of this project. I don't know what I would have done without her help when I moved back to Portugal in the fall of 2003 with my three cats, and then again when I came back to America in the spring of 2005. Without Rosetta, this book would never have materialized. Her support and feedback throughout the writing process really kept me going.

Thanks also go to Petra Helm for her insights and encouraging feedback, and for writing the foreword to this book. Although we've never met, and an entire ocean separates us, our shared love for the work of Alice Miller brings us together in spite of the physical distance.

Raymond Lambert is another person who shares my passion for the work of Alice Miller and I'm so grateful that he's "in this boat" with me. Words can't express how excited I am that he gave me permission to use the Alice Miller painting he owns for my cover. This uplifting image — *Under a Canopy of Heavenly Pink* — has never been seen before in public, and it comes from a time in Alice Miller's life when she was happy and free.

Also, I'd like to give special thanks to Liliane R. for taking the time to read my manuscript and for her very valuable feedback. I am forever grateful to her.

If you're reading this section after reading the main part of the book, you know all about my turbulent relationships with various family members. Despite all the problems, I still owe my brothers and sisters a debt of gratitude. They pushed me out of the family so I could find my true self.

I want to thank my sister Elza for all her support over the years, especially for signing my financial responsibility form so I could come to America. Getting her encouragement to write this book has meant a lot to me.

My sister Laura's support of this project is also quite meaningful, and deeply appreciated.

Laura's daughter, Clara Pennafort, has been a welcome source of friendship, emotional honesty and support. Her feedback has been very encouraging.

I also need to thank my niece-in-law, Fernanda, for having the courage to reach out to me to help her with her beautiful son. Working with her and her son helped inspire me to write this book in an effort to help more young mothers get the right information to become conscious parents.

I get inspiration on a daily basis from my readers online. They share their heartfelt stories and encourage me to continue speaking out for the repressed children inside billions of people around the world. I learn so much from them, and their letters motivate me to keep writing.

The production of this book would not have been possible without a dedicated team of professionals who treated this project as if it was the most important book they've ever worked on. Thanks to Adrienne Silverman and Carol Harangody for their fresh eyes in the editing process.

And lastly, I'd like to thank all the Indiegogo supporters who generously contributed funds to turn my manuscript into the book you're reading now.

Rosetta Fricano, who I mentioned earlier, gave me such a generous contribution that it blew me away. Without her friendship and support over the years this book would never have been possible! She really does mean the world to me and I can't wait to see what adventures the future holds for the two of us together.

Clara Pennafort, my niece who I mentioned above, also came through in a big way for me through Indiegogo. She is one of the few members of the family who understands the fundamental truths I talk about. Her generous contribution filled me with gratitude and I wish her all the happiness and freedom in the world.

Elza Fernandes, my sister, surprised me with an extremely generous contribution that brought my campaign a lot closer to the finish line. Her courage to support my book is astonishing, and it means the world to me. We've had our differences in the past, but without her support over the years I would never have grown into the woman I've become or ever considered writing a book.

Steve McMillian really surprised me with a most generous contribution to help me turn my book into a reality. He is the nicest and sexiest UPS driver in the world and I wish he had my route more often!

Tim Kelly has been a source of support and encouragement for the past nine years. His friendship means the world to me, and his heartfelt contribution on the first day of my Indiegogo campaign really helped get the project off the ground. I am so glad to have his confidence.

Pamela Howland is another person who came through for me in a big way. She was one of the very few people in Scottsdale to have the courage to face the fundamental truths I talk about, and I miss our intense conversations. Her very generous contribution early in the campaign was a big boost to make it a success.

In addition to the six people I just singled out, I want to thank everyone else who helped me raise the resources I needed to publish this book through my Indiegogo campaign. These brave and generous people are: Manuel Arceo, Mickey Berenberg, Steven Beschloss, François Bolduc-Belliard, Sandi J. Boyd, Vince and Rayleen Colletti, Lauren Dawson, Jeff and Sharon Dickinson, Matthew Sharp Fera, Jerry Fielding, Sophia Garrett, Gino Gianneschi, Carrie Hannay, Jan and Sharon Haugen, Cody Hayes, Karen Heard, Perry Herst, Alex Hubert, Bruce C. Jonas, John B. Keats, Laurie Kendall, Mohamed Klach, Raymond Lambert, Bev and Buz Nason, Mark Orr, Joey Robert Parks, Tiago Patacas, Brenda Penwell, Elliot Posner, Frank and Deborah Puglessi, Marco Rösler, Sue Ross, Ester Santos, Ernest H. and Yasuko Y. Shrenzel, Adrienne Silverman, Fernanda Soares, Gary and Sunny Sundine, Paul Svancara, Ed and Kim Sweet, Francis Sweet, Diana Timmerman, Lucia Vaz Bassing, Roger Weber, John Wilwerding, and Eugene and Deborah Zweiback. I thank you from the bottom of my heart and hope you experience true liberation in your lives!

And finally, I want to thank you for reading this book. Alice Miller saved my life, and I hope that through my story, she can save yours, too.

www.ingramcontent.com/pod-product-compliance
Lightning Source LLC
Chambersburg PA
CBHW050441290526
45786CB00006B/2117